PRAISE FOR **HOPE**

It is not easy to make oneself a channel for a great love. So many of us spend much of life rejecting love within ourselves for multiple reasons. Rev. Arica King, in her book, "Hope," lets the love in and we all benefit from what is shared. A spiritual perspective in modern voice that touches upon everything from the primordial to the political present to life and consciousness beyond current human conception, and more. This sharing speaks to my heart. I am impressed not only with the quality of much of what is shared, but by the opportunity to gleam into this courageous and inspired woman as well."

Rev. Josh Reeves, Lead Minister
Mile Hi Church, Lakewood, Colorado

H O P E

Jesus *Speaks*
to Modern America and the World

RECEIVED BY

ARICA ELLEN KING

HOPE: Jesus Speaks to Modern America and the World

Awakening Souls

Published by Awakening Souls LLC
Denver, Colorado
United States of America

ISBN: 979-8-9917407-0-8 (paperback)

ISBN: 979-8-9917407-1-5 (eBook)

ISBN: 979-8-9917407-2-2 (Hardcover)

ISBN: 979-8-9917407-3-9 (audiobook)

Library of Congress Control Number: 2024922398

Editor: Claire Sanders/clairesanders.uk

Cover design and interior formatting:
Mark Thomas/coverness.com

Table of Contents

READER'S PRAYER[1]

[Reading this prayer or offering a similar one is suggested before beginning to read this book and before each subsequent reading session.]

Dearest Father/Mother God [or your most personalized and loving name for God],

I acknowledge that You are with me now, as you are always. You guide me into whatever experiences are the most beneficial for me. I know that You are Love and loving, and that I am loved by You. While I have seen some of my experiences as painful and happening to me, I let in the possibility that they have all been for me and my growth.

I request that You be with me as I read this book and consider its contents. I give You permission to open my heart to truly letting in truths that will awaken me to my becoming who I am and as I have been created to be.

I give You permission to remove or cut all chords or

---

1   Written by receiver, Arica Ellen King. See "Chapter 12, What is Next?", for more information about prayers.

other binders that hold me back from being as I am meant to be regardless of when, how or why the cords were created, whether the binders are ones I placed upon myself out of fear, what I was taught, or otherwise acquired. I now open my heart fully to the greater truths I may have misunderstood or even feared earlier. I am ready to let in the fullest experience of my oneness with You.

Thank You for those experiences that have brought me to this opportunity to bring my understanding of You and my relationship with You to an even deeper level. Thank You for your ongoing and unconditional Love. I open myself and let in Your Love. I look forward to truly knowing that You are with me as I go about my life. I close this prayer knowing that through it, to be open to Your being with me is my permission to help me change in any ways needed. It now is and will forever be. My heart is open.

And so it is.

Amen.

RECEIVER, ARICA ELLEN KING'S PRAYER[2]

Dear God, I surrender my talents and abilities to the purposes of love.

Make me an instrument of peace and love.

May my work become my ministry.

May all I have and do be used for You.

Thus, shall I experience the joy of knowing that what I do is for a higher cause than my mortal mind can even know.

Amen.

---

2 Adapted from a Marianne Williamson morning meditation.

PREFACE

It is I, the one known as Jesus. Did you forget who I AM? I AM Jesus. I am provocative, not to harm you in any way but to get you to realize that you harm yourselves with your thoughts. ... There is fear there. Know that I do this out of love because I want you to be free.[3]

Jesus through Richard Curtis Greathouse

Beloved and holy friends, I come forth to join with you, not from a place that is apart from where you are, but from that place in which we are eternally joined as one Mind, one Heart, one Truth, one Creation, one Love. I come forth, then, to abide with you from the place in which you dwell eternally. I come forth to abide with you because I love you. I come forth to abide with you because you are as I am — the thought of Love in form.[4]

Jeshua ben Joseph (Jesus)
*(may also be spelled **Yeshua ben Yosef**)*

---

3   From "*Soul in the Driver's Seat: A Course in Miracles for the New Age*"
4   From "It is Now Up to You" in *The Way of Mastery.*

This book is not meant to be a book on spiritual or religious doctrine. It is to be short enough to be more appealing to readers as it addresses current social issues in the world with just enough doctrinal information to explain and justify its positions. Within this book, words from Jesus will be shown in a standard font; *materials by the Receiver, Arica Ellen King, will be shown in an italic font. Later editing additions for clarity, etcetera are also enclosed in brackets, [ ].*

This is to give hope to you and others for your future. Whether the future is scary or not, or how long it will take to get there is up to you, and how you and others respond to this.

The words here can lift and inspire you whether this is, as claimed to be from Jesus (Jeshua ben Joseph), does not really matter. Look for the truth in your Heart! That is where credibility must be established, not from any person claiming authority to speak for me or God. Jesus.

Note for Readers: This material was given to Arica with Jesus using "I" to refer to himself and "you" referring individually to the receiver, Arica, in some cases, and generally to readers in most cases. Keeping clarity of who the text applies to has been attempted throughout this work and is shown in different type fonts and with brackets, [ ], for material added after the initial receiving stage.

Chapter 1

SETTING THE STAGE

Have you ever gone for something wholeheartedly and ended up not getting what you went for? Well, I, Arica Ellen King, have, and this book is the culmination of the search that I began over 55 years ago and has continued through today [written May 23, 2024]. Initially, I had a vision that led me to going on a road trip pilgrimage of sorts that left me disappointed and broken emotionally, financially and every other way imaginable when I was 21 years old [in 1968]. Even though I was devastated, I never quit searching for a great connection with God. This story is now a culmination of that quest.

My second, and much more recent, vision now seems related to the first one that started my quest for God connection so many years earlier. It came the night before the U.S. election of November 8, 2016. In that vision I saw and felt as clearly as I have ever felt anything that our country was about to enter a great healing period unlike anything ever before. I took great hope in that vision. When I finally heard the election outcome, I was devastated. How could that be the beginning of a healing period? Not if my political beliefs were correct. Must my beliefs change, are they wrong? "Stay with me for the rest of the story to use a phrase from my father's favorite radio personality, Paul Harvey.

Now, it appears that the great transformation has started. I and you, a reader of this resulting book, can now help bring about the long-awaited transformation of the world.

In the months and now years after that pre-election vision, I have come to realize, perhaps remembering something from my counseling psychology training, that change comes usually, if not always, after a period of resistance. Individually, aspects of one's ego and mind seem to resist change even when you seek it knowing the change will help you. Limiting beliefs and our shadow side (the sides of ourselves we attempt to hide from others and even ourselves) seem impossible to change. Institutionally, the people and organizations that have power and control resist a push for change. The greater the change, the greater the resistance put up against any change by those who would lose control.

I have come to see that the resulting struggle in the United States reveals what was mostly hidden from public awareness earlier. The country is not nearly as united as its name, United States of America, implies. What has happened following the 2016 election is that racial hatred, as well as other areas of social disagreement, have become more acceptable to show publicly. Few knew before then how many subversive and hate-based groups there are. It has become acceptable to express certain sentiments that were previously kept hidden from public view. Is the revealing of how much discord and hatred exists, but had been hidden, the beginning of a healing period? Yes, I now believe so.

Could healing occur when its need was hidden and unknown to most? Can healing the mistrust and hatred previously hidden from public view now proceed? The answers seem obvious now. Objective, unbiased news coverage now openly reveals that there is a great deal of fear, hatred, distrust and divisiveness in our country and the world. I now believe that a healing period is needed and has begun.

My experience receiving and transcribing this book has given me more hope and joy than I imagined possible. It has changed my life regardless of how well this book gets received. The connection I once sought, beginning over 55 years ago, has now come to me in far greater ways than I could have imagined if my wish had been fulfilled when I first sought it. Why that desire to connect with God was not fulfilled years ago when I first had it may be one of those unanswerable "why" questions. I hope that what follows will show you how I can now see that the delay in receiving an answer to my first prayers was a blessing for me. The delay led to my hanging on to that desire for connection after the initial disappointment. Deeper understanding grew in me. Now, the answer to my quest has come.

I now subscribe to the principle that things do not happen to me, but rather happen for me, and that that is true for everyone from a long-term perspective. As I turn the manuscript I wrote into this book, the ultimate third step, things happening through me for others, may now be beginning. The book draft was initially received May 20 to May 22, 2024, at The Awakened School writing retreat for business entrepreneurs gathered to draft books to showcase their expertise. Is this book for business? Only to the extent that my life purpose is to assist in healing the world and that is a legitimate business purpose for me. Or maybe, Jesus took the opportunity presented and his business preempted all my other endeavors. Steve is likely to report that I and my priorities have shifted since I was at the writing retreat.

See for yourself if this book/information gives you as much relief, hope and joy as it gave me when I first began receiving it, and which it continues to give me now every time I think of It, especially when I am working towards getting it out to others. I cannot seem to let it go; I work on it obsessively trying to get it perfect and ready for publication.

This book is for two reasons. First is to show you [*Arica initially, and now everyone*] that I [*Jesus*] am with you [*as with everyone*] now, as I always have been and always will be. You always receive what you most need from me, what is in your highest and greatest interest. You do not need to worry about the how, when, why, or what is in your heart and your goals or mission for where you are. All you need to do is to become open to receiving my direction and to invite in my assistance. You are loved and are supported more fully than you can imagine. Do not fret or worry. I know your desires and what is best for you. You are loved and have been on a long journey through this life preparing you for this. Now you are here and ready. Let go of all your worries, doubts, and expectations.

Secondly, it will be for everyone. Occasionally, you will be used as an example to illustrate how much is known about everyone to demonstrate God's caring. Be open to new material, some you can understand, and some may be beyond your current comprehension. Some will be shared so that you will accept that this did not come from or through you mentally. Your head [*left-brained focus*], with its mental [*analytical*] focus much of the time has served you well in some respects. It has enabled you to survive your 77 years. You have barely scratched the surface of where you can go though.

Unaddressed, but a given in my understanding of who was sharing with me as the receiving began, was that it was Jeshua ben Joseph better known to Americans and most Christians as Jesus. Also unclear is the definition of "soon" used often in the following chapters. My [Arica's] sense is that it could mean months, this earth year, 2024, not many months or years away; or it could mean in a much longer time. The interpretation of "soon" will obviously be understood with greater clarity as the next few months and year(s) unfold. It will be apparent if the fearful controlling interests continue, intensify their efforts, or even gain more power in the next few months, that "soon" does not mean what some would prefer. Do remember that God/ Spirit/Source [That phrase will be mostly used in this book; substitute your preferred name(s) such as Father/Mother God, Holy Spirit/Lord, etcetera, as you wish in the following.] will always ultimately prevail and does not experience time in the human sense and yet, is able to understand it. Think of the Jewish people still waiting for their Messiah and Christians waiting for Jesus' second coming. Both events have been expected imminently for many centuries by some. Perhaps people have been wanting and waiting for the wrong thing. [More about this has been added in the "More About The Timing of This Book" near the end of this book.]

Also note that my return is into peoples' hearts, as I have done for Arica now, and most definitely not as a military, governmental, or religious organization leader who descends from the sky or in some other magical way. The Jews wanted their Messiah to be more than in their hearts; they wanted a military savior to overthrow the Roman control. Boy were they disappointed by me. Religions have certainly distorted the principles they started and perpetuate to control people and their lives. Much more will be said about that.

The actual timing will be seen and understood only as time progresses and you see what happens. Regardless of whether some interpret the coming months as a failure to achieve the anticipated changes rapidly enough, healing and growth will come. Of course, on the human time scale, soon is never fast enough. Those who agree with this material, including the receiver of this, hope soon as used here is based on the human perception of time but that depends on how you and others respond to this and other things/prompts.[5]

---

5 See both the section titled "More About The Timing of This Book" and "Appendix 2 About Recent U.S. Political Developments" for added information regarding the timing of this book's publication.

What role does or will this book have for me [Arica] personally and professionally?

It is to show you that you are capable and have wisdom beyond your conscious understanding. Your expectations are your limits. Remember that time long ago *[my frustrating pilgrimage]* when you were young and went on that road trip expecting to find God? Wisely, God is not as you expected then, so you were disappointed. So, be prepared to get your wishes granted here and now. You are ready at last, which is not to say that it could not have happened earlier. You are ready *[for this]* now. You can do this.

Why me, why this book, why now?

Now because you are finally allowing me/us *[both singular and plural were definitely used; "us" may refer to what some call a cadre of beings including Jesus and other ascended masters or non-physical beings]* to come to and through you at last. You are now open enough. In your past, you have done as you accused your friend and Reiki instructor of doing, having too much of your head or mental thoughts in the process. It has limited you, constrained you to only those options you could mentally imagine. Your friend was graciously modeling you for you to see yourself more so than being herself. *[She was a retired major university departmental head of nursing, so she seemed to be limited by her mental processes, in other words, her traditional medical knowledge.]*

You thought and feared you would be getting a big book to write when you first realized I was with you to write a book. So now, let in big idea information. You are ready, you can get information from me now. You can get my message out. It is time for us to work together to help the world. The world needs the wisdom you have gained and is now coupled with mine. Your loving nature has developed skills. Now you can share with people open to accepting your and my ideas. People are more ready to accept you and the wisdom from and through you than you expect. Many people want and need what you and I have and want to share. Remember and expect that people will be open to you and for you; you are ready for what will be needed. If you were not ready for this, I would not be communicating with you now. You can do what I ask of you. You will do this. I know you are willing and able.

Chapter 2

BEGINNING OF MESSAGE

I [Arica] am ready to receive from you [Jesus]. What are the first few lines I should write?

The world is a mess, it does not understand things nearly as well as you [*Arica*] do. There is so much stress and anxiety in people's lives now that what they are doing can hardly be called living. You have started a book to be written with me that will have an emphasis on what can bring relief to everyone. It will be appropriate for people at all levels, not only for those with certain backgrounds, beliefs, or other characteristics. It will be for everyone. I am here to guide you now more directly.

You have two intangible support resource beings that I will highlight who love and care for you much like I had about 2,000 years ago in your time reckoning. Non-physically, you have been supported throughout your current life by Saint Germain. You recognized it when you saw the violet flame Saint Germain showed you many times as a reminder to be conscious of your circumstances. Saint Germain was my father, Joseph, in his later incarnation leading to my well-known earth lifetime. You are now especially connected energetically with both me, Jeshua ben Joseph, and Saint Germain as you write this with me. You have loved reading and learning about me in recent years. You know of others who have channeled books from me. Now, I choose you to work through and with me. And of course, you know those who are supporting you in your physical dimension including your husband.

Why not you? I know you love me, and I certainly love you and every being, all of God's creation. You have demonstrated that you love me and want to learn more of what I know and demonstrate. So now, you can learn directly from me as you write with me. You are as ready as any of the others who I have written through. So, why not you?

When you show this to Steve, your new husband whose new business he started with you as his partner to support the two of you, he will support you. *[He has been incredibly and fiercely supportive, vastly exceeding my wildest expectations. He asked me to join him in his new business as his business partner in November 2023, then he asked me to marry him days later. We got married on March 16, 2024.]* The two projects, this writing, and his business, need not be incompatible. The two of you are together as a team for very good reasons. I will support Steve too so the two of you do not need to fear what might come.

This work will continue and will answer all your doubts. You are ready to connect with me in greater ways. Your feelings now *[I, Arica, was crying tears of amazement and joy the first several hours of receiving this book and others at the writing retreat saw something special was happening with me.*] are arising because you know this is so, that it can be and is happening and that I am truly who you believe I am, Jesus, you also know as Jeshua ben Joseph. I am asking you to collaborate with me just as I am coming through you now. I also know of your fears of being able to safely get this message out to the world. The reasons for those fears are why this is needed now, and why I am calling on you to work with me. I will, in turn, be there for you. [*Much more on this comes later.*]

Arica, I know that you are loved, and that you are loving. Others have told you they saw your energy as loving long before now. That matches your name, Arica, which means "loving" and Ellen which means "light." They were right about you. The bright light you are scares some people, but not the right people for you, just those people who want to avoid being in the light. You know where to find the right people and have been right to not totally commit yourself to one church/organization or to any one group of people.

Too many people still get caught up in mental and control games. You have questioned whether you have hung on to staying consistently heart connected, not mind focused or mentally and egoic driven since your work using the Big Mind – Big Heart process years ago. You have been correct when you told others that in asking similar questions of themselves, it is a strong clue that they are not guilty of doing as they fear — in other words, it is those who do not question themselves who most often should be examining their actions. Be aware, however, that while questioning oneself may be done for beneficial self-examination, it can also be harmful self-criticism.

Yes, as acknowledged earlier, you have experienced episodes of mental or egoic focus, but you have caught yourself and gotten back on track relatively quickly lately. Keep asking yourself if you are heart centered. There is a reason you loved the Heart-Centered Hypnotherapy approach you were taught years ago.[6] It gave you much and lifted you beyond being stuck in your earlier traumas and helped you to survive challenging circumstances.

Even now you find yourself, in the surprise and joy of connecting with me, wondering where this is going. Well, first I want to show you I know you and that I can lead you to opening to even greater dimensions and visions. And of course, what I say to you applies to everyone.

The people you have connected with previously have not fully understood and seen that the wisdom that comes through you has come through my directing you even though it was mostly unconsciously for you then. You even told people you are not psychic but hope that they find wisdom in what you share. Your insights are Christ wisdom in the greater sense — that "Christ" is a title indicative of a level of connection with God/Spirit/Source, not my or a name. My wisdom, when I lived the life I am most noted for, was and could also be labeled as God/Spirit/Source wisdom. That is wisdom, more than anything else, from sources [*God, Jesus (me), Angels, Ascended Masters, Holy Spirit,*

---

6   Heart-Centered Hypnotherapy is a specific type of regression hypnotherapy taught at the Wellness Institute, Issaquah, WA. I, Arica, was taught Advanced Heart-Centered Hypnotherapy by its developer from 2009 through 2010. It changed my life.

etcetera] upon which you can rely. It never ever leads to anyone, or anything, ever being harmed.

Some of what is in the *Bible*, in its many variations, are distorted ideas. Many have corrupted it over the centuries, creating many versions of it — way beyond just different language translations. Sections with great truths have been omitted because someone did not want others to know the deep truths of what was there (mostly about the oneness of humans with God and clergy not being needed to connect with God), not to simplify and shorten the *Bible* such as has been done for children and youth. Changes to the *Bible* are mostly made to gain power and control others. The additions and changes usually turn away from true spiritual purposes entirely. When you look, you can see that, you know that. That is part of why there are contradictory verses.

Additions and misstatements added to the *Bible* include statements that have become the source of great hatred directed towards some individuals and groups, especially towards those now labeled/identified as gay, lesbian and transgender, whose purpose in life is to show to the world the value of diversity and lead it to its natural changes. Arica, you understand that having experienced versions of it as a transgender person. As noted in your [*Arica's*] recent [*March 16, 2024*] wedding ceremony, 1 John 4:6 – 7 shares that God is Love and that those who judge, and are hateful and persecute, know not God for they do not live Love. From the recent ACIM sequel, *Soul in the Driver's Seat – A Course in Miracles for the New Age* that is stated as "Love does not judge or attack anything. Judgment and attack are in the realm of ego, not soul."

Your recent interest has been in learning more about my life on Earth and even more so in what I taught, not the historical details. What I was about, who I was and what I talked about and demonstrated have your passion. You are right to want to learn more about Truth, not just the historical details. The details do help you and others see that there is credibility and consistency in what happened and is being reported about me as an Essene [*somewhat like mystic Judaism, not a traditional Jew*]. The reports about me in the *Bible* have some basic underlying credibility, even though some of it is very distorted. Some records have even been hidden away because they do not support a church or official's approved messaging.

Also, people describing things happening interpret them based on their own expectations and past experiences. Multiple people observing the same thing often report what they witnessed quite differently. Crime investigators certainly know that each witness sees things through their own eyes and with their own perspective even when they have no intent to distort the facts. You [*Arica*] do this too, though in your not remembering many details, you stay more focused on the bigger perspective than most people.

You are still wondering where this connection and communication is going — how far it will go and how long it will last. That is up to you though if you stay with my intent, it will be a big-time event. Since you see the stress, cost, and limits to others clearly (even though you wanted me to say partially), it should lessen your concern since you will have control over how extensive this book becomes.

This is not meant to be a book on spiritual or religious doctrine. It is to be short enough to be appealing to readers by primarily addressing current issues in your world. It is to touch on principles just enough to justify the positions it takes. It is to give hope for the future. Whether the future is scary, or not, is up to each reader.

The direction I would like to go is different than the books received or channeled from me earlier. Those books began with *A Course in Miracles (ACIM])* that came out in the 1970s. More recent, but lesser-known sequels to *ACIM* are *A Course of Love, The Way of Mastery, A Journey into the Unknown,* and *Soul in the Driver's Seat: A Course in Miracles for the New Age. [The last two are available online only at the time this was written.]*

I know your having read the channeled books listed above adds to your anxiety. What are you are being asked to start, considering how large they are, and with the other books already out, what else can you add? Each of the receivers reaches a certain niche of the total readership potential. How a certain style of writing appeals to some is why, as you wonder, some stay so attached to *A Course in Miracles*, and choose to not move on to the more recent and updated sequels. Those staying with ACIM are not wrong in feeling all they need can be found in the one book though exploring other of my writings would certainly not hurt them. A variety in how things are said, and a more modern language appeals to you, and many others.

But more importantly, none of them share directly about what is up in your society now, how so much being done is claimed to be in my name, and yet quite contrary to my teachings. They clarify and amplify my teaching, but do not focus on societal issues and how my teachings are being misrepresented. Several who claim to represent me, and even speak for me, are an anthesis to my teachings. Remember the warning in the *Bible* for anti-Christs. Many people are being fooled.

Many who say they follow me and call themselves Christians figuratively cheer me on when they hear the story of when I was overturning tables in the temple. Are they ready to hear what I feel about what many who say they are religious and speak for me are doing using my name now? I do not think so. In their hearts they know what is being done is wrong. I am likely to anger many people with what I have to say about your modern world now. You [*Arica*] have learned how to connect with people holding a variety of beliefs, as well as showing your courage in stepping out into living as yourself without fear holding you back.

Also, with your background in several sciences [*chemistry and physics primarily*] and with your contribution that revolutionized research on the Earth's greenhouse warming. [*A 25-page article in National Geographic failed to credit Arica for developing the test method the oceanographers used to gather their data.*] Your language as you understand me can reach a different group of people. I will help them find you and this work. Many inwardly long to hear from someone speaking their language about subjects they cannot address for fear of losing their technical credibility. You know what it is like to be mentally focused, and yet you have known in your heart there is something more.

You also know many are denying science's value to the world

while others are using some scientific knowledge to harm Gaia, the Earth, for selfish reasons. Dire consequences are already beginning to occur on the Earth. You also see how political opportunists are undermining society. Your knowledge and vision are needed these days for multiple reasons. That is why I ask you to join me on behalf of the world as we know it. And no, that is not an exaggeration, and yes, you are in the best position to help me get Truth and justice acknowledged.

Many in the sciences and other technical fields are not fully ego and control driven. They care as you do, but just do not know where to turn to overcome egoic and controlling individuals. Their careers could be jeopardized. Remember, you once started thinking and writing[7] about how individuals can shift from being only mentally driven, to sensing and operating more wholly from their hearts. I, Jeshua, can speak through you and, in a sense, use your words to reach them.

Remember your acquaintance, another hypnotherapist, who with no background in any technical field, authored a book about unifying science and mysticism. It fell flat for obvious reasons — he did not know the world he was trying to address and did not use its language to any appreciable degree. And that is related to why you do not like the language I, Jesus, used in *A Course in Miracles (ACIM)*.

The receiver of *A Course in Miracles, [ACIM was published in 1976]*, expected and needed to receive it in language that

---

7   See "Status of Other Writings by Arica Ellen King" for more about this.

was culturally expected — sounding a bit *Bible* like since that was the background for the receiver and most of those open to spirituality in the United States of the 1970s when it was received and initially shared. Now, so many *A Course in Miracles* students are so attached to its language and style that they will not even consider reading one of the sequels, each with their different "flavors."

Go back in your memory to the pilgrimage road trip you took. You went to the location where the golden plates that became the book now called *The Book of Morman* were found. It told the story of my visit to the Americas following my crucifixion, the story of people who heard my message and began to live by it. That society then lived in peace for about 1,000 years before it forgot what I taught, and the peaceful era ended. That sort of peaceful era is what I am asking you to help me create now, 1,000+ years of peace.

Anticipating that that magnitude of change (literally Heaven on Earth) is what I am asking you to help bring about. It is possible and even likely to occur in a far shorter time than you imagine. After all, the *Book of Mormon* story reported that I was with the people then for 40 days after my crucifixion. As in the ancient Americas, when people hear the Truth, change can come about very quickly. That magnitude of change happened quickly then. You can help me bring that about now!

Try to imagine now what will happen when your society makes such a change. The book you have been working on [*How to Change: Finding and Moving into L.O.V.E. (Living One's Vital Essence)*], is about personal change. You can and should publish it soon even though where it leads will be nothing compared to the societal changes you will be working towards if you join me and get this book out to the world. Individuals will still need your wisdom on how to make desired personal changes and others will want to learn more about you and your perspectives.

What a change it will be when all the divisiveness and warring in the world ends. News coverage has focused on sensational, emotion-generating stories appealing to individuals expecting to hear reports on suffering. [*News consumers are taught to expect and want bad news.*] Remember the contrast with the non-feeling-based report by Robert Reich you [*Arica*] read recently. When people begin to not live in fear, they will understand how the stories shared reach and affect people through the feelings they created. In your world, the predominant feeling now is fear. Fear, even for one's life, exists in some areas and especially for some races, identities, and religions. You [*Arica*] personally, have not been caught up in fear even though many who share your [*transgender*][8] identity are even killed for being who they are relatively frequently. How Christian is that? Yet, you and other [*transgender*] individuals are a subset of humans whose mission

---

8 The original description of the receiver was the deliberately vague "identity" without the adjective "transgender." Jesus left it up to Arica to choose how self-disclosing she chose to be. Appropriate modifications in the following text were approved by Jesus. More on this topic will follow in Chapter 12. The disclosure was chosen so that this book can be seen as an example of moving away from fear-based living. It was chosen out of love and wanting to help change the world as intended by Jesus. Candor also leads to more empathic understanding and credibility.

in life is to help prepare the world for upcoming natural changes.

Your identity is very misunderstood because most are afraid of change. You have personally avoided almost all versions of violence directed towards others like you. You have chosen to only travel to selected places very appropriately and wisely. Not everyone can choose to live as wisely as you have, however. Please note that your safety has come, at least in part, by my being with you and guiding you. You did not have to live in fear for your life as some you have worked with have had to and still do. You have lived safely despite your gender and hair color thanks to me, to put it bluntly. I have watched over you far more than you imagine. You are different in having started your spiritual questing years ago. You avoid traveling in areas where those who are threatened by others for their being different is likely. Unfortunately, the risk in areas in which you travel is still not zero. [*This paragraph was left as received, and not modified following the identity disclosure preceding it.*]

So now, you are beginning to wonder again how what I am asking you to join me in doing will impact you and Steve. And you cannot imagine the ultimate impact on the world this can have, not just changing its power structure, but changing it into a peace-loving, non-divisive world with Heaven on Earth.

For you personally, know that this will not just be a shock to you, but as you expect, to Steve too. Be gentle with him, give him time to adjust. You have had the surprise of receiving this directly from me. Steve will hear about it secondhand from you. I will be with you and Steve as you share the news of this book you are to publish. Remember that Steve has been worried about how he can help support the two of you in continuing what you have been doing. So of course, his agreement, not just yours, is important. Steve's first response is likely to be: "How can we do that? What must change?"

The short, more immediate answer is simpler for you as you know and feel the energy of being with me as you write this, while Steve has not as consciously or knowingly had that support from me. In the long term, much can and will change. Fortunately, not just in ways that frighten you, but for the better also. You will need to see that too before you can truly believe me. You will have to use two words I know you have hated and considered a terrible way on which to base a life, "belief" and "trust." [*Arica prefers knowing something over faith or believing in something having experienced a degree of knowing.*] Will you trust me? It is about changing you and your perspectives before it becomes about changing others. I am speaking through your heart now only because you have opened yourself to me.

Again, remember your pilgrimage road trip search and how you have told many people since then that you were born into a family whose church taught that God is not dead, God still speaks to people now, not just in Biblical times. You have your background from your childhood plus you have become a great deal more informed in your adult years. Your life, as you have begun to see, has been all about growth and change. Your reasonable, rational-based approach will reach Steve, and as you will come to see later, many many more people.

And remember your reading Rasha's book and how you loved

and envied her, especially in her *Journey to Oneness* that we, you [*Arica*] and I [*Jesus*], are loosely modeling the structure of this book on. You too have a journey you are undertaking. I will be with you and Steve throughout it. Steve, being your supporter will also be a big part of this. Go ahead and finish the book[9] on which you have been working. It will give you credibility and help people who follow you. Yes, there are some who have already found you and there will be more, many more wanting to follow your work once they learn of it. Now, you are ready to begin the real writing work since you have accepted that I am who I claim to be, and you have agreed to collaborate with me. [*See the chapter titled "Afterword" for more about Steve's reaction to Arica's news and what has changed for both of them.*]

---

9   *How to Change: Finding and Moving into L.O.V.E. (Living One's Vital Essence).* See the "Status of Other Writings by Arica" listed at the end of this book.

Chapter 3

FIRST STEPS

Tell me [Arica] again, what is this book to be about.

It will be on two primary levels for our purposes. One is to first show you [*Arica*] that you are important and are growing and contributing to the world, not just surviving or existing. You have your energy and wisdom which are of great value to the world. So first, I will endeavor to build you up, not only in your eyes, but for the world to understand you are special and an asset collaborating with me, Jesus [*also known as Jeshua ben Joseph*]. You know I love you. My telling you about yourself is not just to build you up, it is also to demonstrate to others, readers of this, that I know and love them as well as I know and love you.

Second, in the face of society's divisiveness of recent years, people want and need relief. Peace is urgently being called for now, not some later time. The focus here will go towards healing the world by calling on everyone to remember what is important and True and to BE themselves. Yes, you reader(s), have the task of making a choice as to whether to stay where you have been, or to take a risk and go for Truth, peace, and happiness. Staying in a comfortable but limiting zone does not lead to real happiness.

Yes, this will lead to changes that are unimaginable for you now — but ones you will never regret making. As you look back on your life, it now appears to you as a flow toward something even though there were periods that were not just uncomfortable, but painful and did not seem at all purposeful. Many times, it felt fragmented and directionless. Now you see that they have led you to being where and who you are today. And you are happy with that, with who you are now, with who you have become.

Those who know you, including Rachael Jayne Groover, whose support led to your writing this book, and those who have seen the potential and future in you will be thrilled to see you in this work. Rachael Jayne came into your life somewhat unexpectedly for a reason, including getting you started writing what turned out to being this book. Earlier she saw your potential clearer than you did after you first saw her for who she is and what she is doing. Previously, you had wondered what her true motives are. After all, can you explain the writing retreat where this was written as a business retreat? So, continue to allow your trust in yourself and others to grow. What is to come will come naturally, and in some respects, seemingly effortlessly. When you feel the need to try to force something, that is evidence that you are back into your head space/mental/ego, etcetera. Growth, as well as contributing to others, will not be about anything requiring force. Remember that simple does not mean easy though.

Chapter 4

HISTORY AND SOCIAL ISSUES

Learn from the experience of the United States in recent years. Divisiveness does not help; it harms people. Divisiveness does not allow growth; it tears people down. Enough people are finally growing in consciousness to create some movement towards electing a principled government[10], one that promotes a sane, rational U.S. government and eventually, others throughout the world. Marianne Williamson worked towards this in her promotion of the ACIM book initially, and then in her becoming a U.S. presidential candidate. She did not gain enough support. Too many people did not see the bigger picture of where Marianne Williamson attempted to lead them. Few see how achieving a principle-based peaceful society could come

---

10   See "Appendix 2: About Recent U.S. Political Developments Part 4 The November 5, 2024 U.S. Election Outcome."

about as many powerful leaders selfishly resisted her efforts. Her ideas were good, but they were before enough people were ready for them. The ideas shared in this book will be seen as very radical initially. The radical, thought-provoking ideas will come to be understood eventually as people gain hope and learn who they really are and why they are on planet Earth.

Change is frightening to everyone. That is part of why you succumb to the traps of comfort zones. Those threatened by their losing power are especially afraid of change. Eventually, most humans will come to welcome the wisdom of living in a world filled with love and peace, rather than the divisiveness of the "us versus them" mentality that there has been. Divisiveness has been fed by a few taking advantage of many. The masses have recognized that change is needed but are limited in their understanding of how to achieve it. They have been deceived into supporting divisiveness and hatred as the way to achieve needed changes. Those with some power have created changes that further empowered themselves and others like them instead of helping those they fooled into helping them gain power. Controlling people have not seen how a peaceful and stable world can come about and even help them too. Vilifying and divisive weakening of those perceived as outsiders or opponents cannot heal or ever lead to peace. Society will come to see how much harm has been done and then, and only then, will it ultimately become ready to heal and have peace.

Remember your [Arica's] vision the night before Donald Trump was elected in the November 8, 2016, election? You saw that a great healing period was about to start. You did not understand how that could be the start of a healing period when you then heard the election outcome. You have seen all the chaos that has followed. It has become those in power resisting letting go of their power and not wanting any change other than reinforcing their own power. Many have chosen power over principles they used to stand for.

It became ironic that the 2016 U.S. election was a vote for change, but the change it brought about gave power to one seeking power selfishly rather than helping create the changes the non-elites wanted and need. Some people now love to hate Donald Trump. Note the irony and inconsistency in those words. Yes, he has a soul and is in fact serving the world by playing the role that reveals how much hatred and misunderstanding there is in your world. Indeed, seeing where things are and understanding how they got there is a necessary first step in the healing that is needed. Healing will come as hatred is understood.

The extreme self-centered leadership style that has followed the 2016 election is antithetical to democratic principles. People have seen no other way to push for the change they need, but those in power have been too entrenched, too powerful. So, the electorate got change, but instead of what they wanted, they got change that ironically, further entrenched and enriched the powerful elitists. It was not a change that was beneficial for the majority who fought for and needed it. Society is learning its lesson now and is moving towards being ready for a new, principled leadership.

While there are those who will resist and deny that you [*Arica*] speak for me, or even that I could speak through you, or anyone, Truth will ultimately prevail. The movement towards favoring a fascist or other dictatorial-style leadership will fail as people realize it only harms them and does not lead to stability, much less true peace. Those striving for power always work to increase their power and control and always encounter opposition from those who want the power for themselves. That does not lead to peace or happiness for anyone.

What you will share through me will become an obvious answer to what ails your society. Resistance from those who have power and control, including your religious institutions, will melt away in the face of the population's determined resistance to continued selfish leadership and control. Divine wisdom that will be shared from me through you and the wisdom you have developed in your quest for growth and understanding can and will create this. It will have that much power.

And yes, I hear your silent prayer that you do not get turned into one seeking power or glory for yourself.

Yes, you have trepidations of the upcoming election, 2024, and if wisdom will come forth in it. Do not be troubled, know that Spirit is alive and well, and is doing its part working to heal what ails your country and the world in general. You also have other entities working to serve the world's needs, to protect it. Positive change will happen as fast as it can but only when people are ready for it. The United States is not the only country or political division that is fragmented and divisive, filled with fear and hatred. Think of the world and how peaceful people and countries can have sanity prevail. The population in previously selfishly led, powerful-interest countries will lead to profound changes as they learn of my True teachings.

Go back to your vision of a period of healing being brought in by the 2016 election. People must realize that change is always resisted by those who have power. Power loves being in control. So, what are the changes people can anticipate now or soon? Corporate leaders and others in the elite class now have enormous power, they create many of the laws. Elon Musk at Tesla, for example, can command an income of almost fifty billion dollars a year. Is he that much more creative or a better business leader? Frankly, no. Nor is any other executive paid so enormously beyond what was once the norm.

Do you remember the days when it was said that the most valuable asset a company has is its employees? That belief can come back. How far and how fast it returns is up to the citizenry and who they elect as the next leaders. The upcoming U.S. election [2024] will determine much — how much healing of hatred remains to be done as the extent of discord is revealed.

Chapter 5

YOUR HOME, GAIA

You should not be surprised that abusing the Earth harms everyone now and for years to come. It should frighten you. You [*Arica and all beings*] are a part of God and so you have all of God's potential within you. You [*Arica*] know of the butterfly effect where something seemingly so minor as a butterfly flapping its wings on one side of the world can have major effects on the other side of the world.

Your home, Earth, is suffering. Human suffering caused by human environmental abuse is leading towards the Earth becoming less hospitable for humans and harmful to many life forms is well documented. Earth has a spirit as do you. Earth's spirit name is Gaia, given by those who are connected with and listen to Earth's spirit. They are correct in their worries for your planet. Many Indigenous peoples have connected with the Earth and know that is true. The Earth can recover, but thanks to the denial and resistance there has been, the cost of helping Gaia recover will be greater, far greater, than the cost would have been if the damage had been halted earlier, or never done. And now, some proposed technical remedies are likely to make things worse, not better as they attempt to mitigate the harm rather than stop the harm being done. Many of those who insisted there was nothing to worry about years ago knew that was not true; they just wanted to maximize their profits and minimize their responsibilities. Who does not know that it is more difficult and costly to repair damage than to prevent damage before it occurs? That is why you do preventive maintenance on your vehicles, for example.

Bluntly, your planet is being abused and otherwise made less habitable by those who seek to benefit from it without compensating for or doing restoration or remediation for the damage they cause to it. There are many reports showing how serious the damage has become. There is a price to pay for harming your Earth home. It can absorb only so much, and it has long since passed that limit. Those who have selfishly denied the harm they are causing must no longer benefit from doing so. They must pay the cost of remediation, and not delay it or be allowed to shift the cost to another time or to other people. The time to care for the Earth is now.

The abuse should have ended years and years ago when scientists first warned of the harm being done, or even better, was never allowed. The Earth is now at a breaking point that must not be denied any longer. Stopping the harm can no longer be postponed without catastrophic results. You know that; you have been warned. There is only so much abuse the Earth can endure before it takes its own serious actions to protect itself.

As has been said, inhabitants of Earth have no Planet B option available. That of course ignores that the Earth is not the only place with conscious beings. Accept the reports of wise people, not of this Earth and physical dimensions. You chose to come to the Earth for a reason. It is time everyone acknowledged that and helps take care of your physical home.

Humans are not the only conscious beings on the Earth. Accept the reports that other conscious beings exist not only on this physical Earth in a physical dimension. Humans on the Earth are certainly not the only conscious beings here, and many non-human beings are of a much higher consciousness than imagined.

Anticipate that someday your society will come to see that there are other conscious beings with you on your Earth. Recently, researchers learned that whales have a complicated communication system. Whale and other marine mammals' consciousness is very high. That is known and accepted by many humans.

Do not forget that your so-called pets are beings which have unique gifts they share such as the unconditional love they choose to share with humans. They choose to serve as human pets even though they know that some humans treat them horribly. All animals, in fact, all objects, have a consciousness.

It is recorded in the *Bible* that God created the Earth and gave it to humans for their use. It never meant that they could rape and pillage it recklessly. Humans have always been responsible for their actions. Why should it be any other way? Having stewardship has always meant having responsibilities.

An irresponsible you can do anything approach was never intended. The clear meaning in the *Bible* has been intentionally distorted and made even worse by some with power profiting by Earth's harm.

Chapter 6

WHO ARE YOU?

The external, physical dimensional you is not who you are.

You are fortunate beings because you are individualized expressions of God. You are an eternal, everlasting creation of God/Spirit/Source, the energy that created everything. You are given a creative ability shared with and of God. Your free will, the ability to not see and even deny your oneness with God/Spirit/Source, is a part of that. When you use it wisely, you benefit everyone and everything; if you abuse it, you abuse everyone and everything. Consider the responsibility of that! I was given the title Christ; it is a title, not a name. You too are a Christ whether you know it or not, even if you do not live it. That is as you were created to be.

You, both the receiver and readers of this, every human actually, chose to come to the Earth for a special reason, the growth of your soul. In forgetting who you are you are subjected to being figuratively like a piece of paper getting crumpled and wrinkled or even wadded up. Your life's task is to restore yourself to being the pristine piece of paper you once were. That is how our souls grow.

Continuing with another analogy, many of you like the analogy of God being an ocean of energy. Continuing the analogy further, see that God is like the ocean and you are like droplets of water broken free from the mighty ocean when a wave breaks above the ocean's surface or a water molecule evaporates from it. You, like a droplet of spray above a wave, can never stay entirely away from the ocean. Raindrops, or even miniscule water molecules, wherever they go, eventually return to the ocean. Similarly, separation from God can only be temporary as you grow into recognition that you are a powerful cocreator with God.

Learn who you are and live being who you are. Learn to let go of trying to control everything. Striving to know enough to be in control of all your experiences is hopeless and needless. You can receive all the information and guidance you need through your heart, otherwise called intuitively. Your heart energy (not the physical heart) is vast, way beyond your imagination. When you open your heart, you will receive all the information and guidance you need. You will receive that guidance when you need it as you open yourself up to God. You do not need to do anything to earn God's love. [*or to have a connection with God*]

In birth upon the Earth, you experience separation from God/Spirit/Source; you have a form of amnesia or forgetfulness. You forget who/what you are. You forget who you are because you have free will, the ability to choose to operate as though you are not part of God/Spirit/Source. You have that gift, and yes, it is a gift that you could not have been given. The benefit is by not knowing who you are initially, when you see who and what you are, you get a better appreciation of just how incredible and wonderful you are. That is a gift non-physical and non-humanoid beings never experience.

You chose to come to Earth to experience the opportunity to learn and become who you really are. Many humans have recognized the value of this gift. Poets and mystics, for example, write of it after touching on aspects of it to varying degrees, but can never describe it fully. Experiencing connection with God/Spirit/Source is unfathomable and beyond comprehension so words never describe it adequately. It can be said that you cannot conceive of or comprehend it until you experience it. When your mind is closed to the possibility of intangible or non-physical energies, you shut off its energy and so cannot even know it is there.

Another analogy: You are like a radio which cannot show there are radio waves present until it is turned on and tuned correctly to the energy frequency present. You can tune yourself to become a great receiver once you feel energy showing you that energy is present. Once you tune into the energy frequency, it becomes obvious that the energy is there. You get to experience it by hearing, seeing, or feeling it. You then receive the message or information it has within it.

Many people tune into the energy briefly, then rapidly lose it. Retuning their receptibility after it has been recognized once becomes simpler each subsequent time. The rewards of doing that is why mystics do all sorts of things to try to tune in and stay tuned in to the God signal. Each time you succeed, it becomes easier, and when it is lost, returning is usually both easier and faster. Expecting to be connected 100% of the time is an unreasonable expectation and is not required.

Connecting with universal energy is why some people have managed to write with great wisdom. Once you connect with the energy, you learn how to better maintain that connection and how to reconnect if you lose the connection. A fitting example comes from more recent times since things from the distant past often get edited, deleted, or otherwise altered over time. The prolific writing of Ernest Holmes who established Religious Science, also known as Science of Mind, illustrates writing with intuitive knowing. He did not claim to be writing through channeling, just through his understanding. The key to evaluating any form of spirituality is to look at how it empowers you to discover the power within you. If an authority is telling you what to believe, it should be seen as not likely to be for you as it is for them. Your inborn task is to find the truth within yourself. Again, anything giving you interpretations of what to believe or do is not likely to be for who you are and in your best interest.

The "magic" test for if a belief is based on Truth is: Does it harm anyone or anything? If it can cause any harm, it is not of God/Spirit/Source. God/Spirit/Source would never harm anyone or anything. That is an absolute Truth, and yes, there are absolute truths. Many things may be relative, but not everything. Some things are absolute. All absolute truths can be found by careful examination of anything regardless of how simple it might appear outwardly.

Another detail that aids examination of principles is that everything is ultimately simple. That does not mean it is easy to do, however. Scientists and mathematicians can develop eloquent equations that reveal and often predict interactions not previously known or understood. An example developed by Albert Einstein is $E=mc^2$ It changed your world as it revealed nuclear power potential. The mathematics involved might be unintelligible to non-mathematicians, but simple to mathematicians. Simple, beautiful concepts are the ultimate explanation. People often look for oversimplified black and white explanations reflecting their limits of understanding. Your world mostly has shades of gray; it is not just black or white. The following sections will touch on this more.

Chapter 7

ABOUT SCIENCE

Two examples of the conflict between science and religion are the controversy over the role of evolution in the development of life and the theories on the origin of the universe. The alleged conflict is discussed in the following.

There are those who try to tell you that the Earth is just over 6,000 years old, and that humans and dinosaurs co-existed. That is totally false. It would be more plausible to believe that dinosaurs never existed, yet creationists usually admit that they did exist at one time. You know that is proven wrong by your sciences in many independent, reproducible ways. Those who claim that science is wrong and believe that the Earth is only about 6,000 years old do not just not accept science and what it tells us. They deny the wisdom and capability of God/Spirit/ Source by believing it must be as simple as what they are capable of understanding. They do not understand the creative energy of God/Spirit/Source. Understanding is limited by not looking beyond what has been written in the *Bible*. Much of the *Bible* was written symbolically, and never intended to be taken literally.

Most advocates for evolution know that there is a divine intelligence guiding creation that got life started and continues, but the topic of evolution has been made so controversial by Biblical creationists, that discussion is largely reduced to evolution vs. creationism in almost all circumstances. Knowledgeable people have been forced to say evolution is the only creative force to discount the absurdity of claims that the Earth is only about 6,000 years old. Consider that there are historical remnants of civilizations that are thousands of years older than that, even about 50,000 years in at least one case. Geologic evidence is that the Earth is over 4.5 billion years old.

Scientists find that organisms and animals sometimes change so shockingly rapidly, beyond what unguided or random evolution could explain, that creative intelligence and forces must be acknowledged. So, science acknowledges that there are non-random creative forces as well as slower evolutionary progression.

The other common example of the controversy between science and religion is science telling us that the age of the universe is about 13.8 billion years old [*number's range has varied some as science's dating methods advanced but not drastically*], and that it started with what is called a "big bang" that can be explained mathematically. That was the inspiration for the name of the popular TV show *The Big Bang Theory* that continues to be rebroadcast in reruns.

It all gets down to what created the stuff that exploded in

or was created by the big bang. It was the creativity of God/Spirit/Source of course. The creative force has continued to operate and guide the development of the physical world while it continues to lead development in both tangible and intangible dimensions. You [*Arica and knowledgeable readers*] know this. It is obvious to all willing to look for reason and logic in the universe.

Again, those who insist science is not correct, and that life can only have been created by God as described in the *Bible* suffer from an extreme under-appreciation of God's creativity expressed through natural laws that God created. Religious leaders' credibility, as well as their egoic sense of their own importance, is further undermined by their insisting that they alone can know God, and that we must trust and have faith that what they tell us is true. Again, their claim that the degree of nature's complexity could only have been God's work, as they understand God, fails to credit God with the capability of creating natural laws that are way beyond their comprehension.

Chapter 8

A CHRISTIAN NATION?

Will many continue to pretend that the United States is a Christian nation, which it has never been in a true sense, or even especially in the sense that those claiming it is these days imply? It allows its citizens to suffer from health issues while every other advanced nation cares for all the people in them, not just its citizens. Ironically, the justification for that is not to save money; the U.S. healthcare system costs much more than it does in other industrialized nations. Who benefits from this system? A few powerful and wealthy individuals and corporations/organizations profit from it.

The United States allows children to suffer from hunger and poverty when it could easily afford to see that they are all fed adequately. Women are now forced to give birth in some U.S. states when they become pregnant, but children are not adequately supported once they are born. All these issues are as advocated by "Christian" nationalists, etcetera. So, is the United States a Christian nation? I do not think so!

Life is sometimes ended by execution, or put in more blunt words, people are killed because they were a wounded person who broke down and harmed another, or others, in their inability to cope with their stress. They do not receive compassion or help for their being broken. What about the tired and hungry referred to on your Statue of Liberty. You do not have a Christian nation at all. The phrase *"E Pluribus Unum"* means "Out of Many, One" is on some of your coins. Is that accepted now? No, not by very many including so-called Christians anymore!

My teachings recorded in the *New Testament* talk of loving one another. The Good Samaritan teaching is a great example of that. Those who advocate that the United States is a Christian Nation will not recognize a true Christian government when one comes; they will probably fight against its formation. Those suffering cannot receive it soon enough. Those in power now do not recognize how marvelous a truly Christian government can be, and how it could benefit them too.

In a society based on love, no one is marginalized. Those who have had power will recognize how much better things are once they accept and adjust to not having unreasonable power and control. Your founding fathers had it right in saying that all men [*people of course, not males only and not just others like themselves*] are created equal. Once those in power see that they achieve nothing without workers, they will reward work equitably. Your world has never experienced that in truth and totality. The world is becoming ready for that. The time is soon!

[The following paragraphs of this chapter were received after the original transcription.]

Your world is full of misunderstandings and misdirection under the guise of being Christian. For example, some of the current U.S. political controversy is focused on eliminating women's access to abortions supposedly in the need to protect the unborn child's right to life. Where is comparable concern for a child's welfare following its birth? Is the real purpose something else such as controlling women? Of course it is!

Also, where is any awareness that a fetus' experience, including its potential future of being aborted, is always as planned by its soul with a cadre of spiritual advisors before it is conceived? Political actions being taken show religious people advocating against abortions do not understand souls [*or democracy and freedom of choice*]. A soul may choose to become an embryo that will not be carried to birth due to natural miscarriage or abortion, for a variety of reasons. Or, a soul may choose to develop from an embryo into a fetus that leads to its birth as a healthy normal human child, or even into a genetically, mentally, or physically imperfect child. God covers all these issues quite well without any need for human intervention or forcing anyone's beliefs on others.

A related question for your consideration: What happens to a child whose spirit knows it was not wanted, that its mother would have chosen to have an abortion rather than have an unplanned child if she could? Hint: The child is usually extremely wounded emotionally and even physically, unlike an aborted fetus's spirit.

Look at the experiences of most who know they were adopted for clues.

Those attempting to inject their religious views into politics commonly feel they should be commended for their devotion to their beliefs and to God. They are wrong. Their zealous actions are often conducted to prove their faith to themselves rather than to help others. They have been taught that promoting their beliefs is God's commandment. In fact, God does not need their zeal. Instead, such zeal usually alienates others and leads to many avoiding religious groups. This misconception comes from very mistaken interpretations of my teachings. No one needs to be saved by being told of and converted to believing in me. God does not punish or judge, God is LOVE; God only honors all his/her/its/their creations. All souls, and all of God's creations are beautiful and loved regardless of who they are and what they believe or do. None would ever be sent to hell or purgatory because they failed to believe in me or call out my name before their last breath. All were created in Love and are loved, never judged, never punished.

The only desired and effective way to properly influence others is by living an exemplary and loving life. That also leads to personal growth, the real goal. The need to convert others is a very mistaken understanding of my teachings, instituted by those who wanted to expand the number of people they could control. That is also why birth control is sometimes opposed. Trying to force or change others' beliefs is never appropriate. Everyone should be free to find what meets their individual needs. Remember your nation's founding fathers added freedom of (and "from" by clear inference) religion. There was a time that was a point of pride in your nation. Pride is pretty universally seen as an undesirable trait. Pride in your country, or something else, is not always pride, but can be appreciation of something of value. The United States does indeed have some things that should be preserved and valued.

In my life I am known for, I called for only acceptance of political rules as required by rulers of that society. Now, people want to rebuild the U.S. government misusing my words and principles as well as history itself. The nationalist focus being advocated is the opposite of what I taught.

Spiritual growth and movement towards a peaceful society do not require a Christian nation, especially not one in which Christianity is as defined by most so-called Christians these days or when it is imposed on others. It could literally be better if no nation were Christian if Christian means as many believe Christian means these days. Consider what I have to say later about Hinduism and Buddhism.

Chapter 9

MORE POLITICAL QUESTIONS

Dearest Jeshua, as you undoubtedly know, I do not know where this writing is going. At times I really do not know what might be next. Each time I felt I had no idea what, if anything is next and slow down writing, suddenly my writing continues essentially uninterrupted, only slowed briefly. I thank you for being with me and invite you to continue. I request that you step in, to continue with me, to relieve any resistance I might have due to fears I might have about how dangerously someone might react to this material or to me personally. And as you know, I am still concerned about how this is happening. It does not matter to me where this communication with me is going. I trust you will be doing the rest through me and for me, as well as with me. So, I will stop my questions, which I now see are really questioning your direction, and I pledge to allow you to continue writing through me from where we paused last night.

There is a great deal of divisiveness and hateful things happening in your world. There are those who are not just not loving others; they denounce, hate and even attack others. They are not being true Christians. Some in your time use my name and their interpretations of me to try to control others. You can and will help me get past the obstacles some have placed in the way of everyone knowing me by attempting to place themselves between us.

People who study the *Bible* know I did not like what was being done in the temples. You cannot imagine how I feel about what is being done supposedly in my name now. It is beyond deceit and abusive to use my name to mislead and gain power over others. Where is the love, acceptance, and compassion for those suffering to be found?

Certainly, not in the hearts of so many religious leaders and their followers these days. It is inconceivable how many things said these days are claimed to be in my name and consistent with my teachings yet are the opposite. How horrifying it is that someone self-centered and power hungry managed to become a leader of your country and claim my support in his seeking to gain power? Is my message confusing? I say no, not at all! It is people deceiving others in their trying to get and hold on to power. There is no religious value in that!

Ever since the movement of trying to remake your nation into a "Christian" nation began, it has moved farther and farther away from anything I stand for. Even though there are many errors and omissions in what is recorded about what I taught, there is no ambiguity in the *Bible's* record of my teachings being about loving one another. True Christian spirit is hard to find in any of the religious movements these days. The politically powerful deceived so many people so well that a large portion of the population who felt like change was needed were tricked. The deceivers then blamed others for their not helping those they had promised to help, beginning what has become a vicious cycle.

Many deceived individuals have become bullies as they accepted the divisive blaming of minorities and others who are misunderstood. The list of maligned groups is growing. The bullies feel justified for being hateful for why they do not get a fair share of the country's prosperity. As more scapegoats are needed, the divisiveness has grown beyond people of color who have always been maligned in your country where their ancestors were legally treated as subhuman and enslaved in some areas. Immigrants and anyone appearing different initially, and now anyone needing assistance such as the poor, elderly, sick, disabled, etcetera are blamed for society's ills and their having needs they cannot meet themselves. The LGBTQ+ community and non-Christians are now also blamed for injustices caused by the powerful controlling interests as the need to further deflect awareness away from the real causes of your society's injustices grows.

Chapter 10

WHO YOU REALLY ARE

Going back to a thought from earlier, God/Spirit/Source's creations endure eternally. You as a spirit are also indestructible, enduring, eternal, or whatever equivalent words you choose to use. My instrument here, my scribe, has experienced moments of insight into this in her contemplating writing a book about a soul's journey.

Meanwhile, getting back to where I was going, you are always free to do as you choose. My receiver here can choose to ignore getting this out publicly or even deny receiving this and destroy this creation before word of it gets out even though some of those at the writing retreat where this is being received already know something unusual is up for you [Arica]. You are quite reasonably fearful of how some might respond to your getting this message out. That is why I promised to protect you, Steve and others who help get this message out to a broad audience. And obviously, I hope you get this out quickly and as effectively as possible to many, many people.

Your world has many individuals who have seen that true joy and happiness come from within. You[*humans*] are not intended to suffer through a torturous life on Earth waiting, hoping, and having to try to earn an eternal reward. The hell to fear is the only one that exists, the one you create and put yourself through during your life on Earth. Life on Earth can literally be made into a hell. Of course, that was never intended. You chose to come into existence on the Earth's physical plane because you [*your soul, the eternal part of you*] know you are love and that you can come into greater realization and manifestation of that Love faster and easier on Earth. Of course, easier, and faster need clarification. Faster is in your three-dimensional time sense since time really does not exist for eternal, non-physical beings. Of course, easier should be in quotes since it is used loosely and ties in with your physical concept of time and effort.

Look at what some humans go through on your Earth. Why do some areas have great abundance and few humans living there need to struggle for food and shelter? Some have many "toys" and other fun things they prize including exotic foods. Others, especially in so-called undeveloped portions of your world, struggle daily for survival. Why would their soul choose such a life for them instead of an easier life in an affluent area? The short answer is that such a life helps their soul's lesson(s) for why they chose to have a life on the Earth's three-dimensional world. It is absolutely not for punishment. You would be far more accurate in assuming that they are beings of higher consciousness rather than thinking that they did something bad in another incarnation and are paying a price for bad karma by having a difficult life.

That question of why such a life would be chosen is, of course, unanswerable from the human mental perspective. There are more reasons that will be explained further in the following.

As shared earlier, you are expressions of love. My receiver has coined the acronym L.O.V.E. for "Living One's Vital Essence" for her other book that is not published yet. Those who serve others learn that in serving, there are great rewards. That is what my receiver has experienced. In serving others, one learns and grows more themselves. The receiver of this learns much more when she serves others. She openly acknowledges that when she shares, she gains more than she gives.

Those whose existence is only physically focused cannot imagine any value in serving and helping others. They focus on taking from others. They will eventually understand how limiting that role is. Then there are those who see that giving and receiving are really the same thing. There cannot be receivers unless there are givers, and there can be no giving if there is no receiving. In this, as in all things, the universe seeks balance.

Some notably advocate for giving as their way to receive more [*tithing and other giving*]. That is not integrous, noble or charity. Giving should be from the heart, wanting to share, not a desire to get more. The universe does not operate like that. Motive does count, not just the outcome. The ends do not justify the means.

Chapter 11

PHYSICAL ENERGETIC EFFECTS

Sound is a powerful energy. It has both healing and destructive potential. Humans speak for many reasons. There are many languages in your world, and most languages have distinct dialects or variations. Each culture or subculture has a collective consciousness or certain energetic pattern that shows up in its language or dialect, and each sound has a certain energy effect. Some languages are described as flowing and rhythmic while others are guttural, etcetera. It has been observed that certain sounds help calm and heal while others promote anger or other strong negatively labeled feelings. Each language and its dialects or accents have their own energies and their effects although there may be some individual variations in a specific sound's effect such as a preference for or an aversion to certain sounds or music. Similarly, music tastes vary reflecting the consciousness expressed.

There is also a collective consciousness for your whole planet as well as variations between regions. Why is that? Everyone is unique and each variation has its sphere of influence. An enormous difference in communication rarely experienced between humans is telepathic communication. It is experienced by very few individuals although all are capable of it when they are heart centered/intuitively connected.

A perspective on sound important to the receiver of this that is less commonly known is called Kirtan. It originated in Hinduism and has been adopted in Buddhist traditions also. In it, it is recognized that the ancient India Sanskrit language maintains more of the original energy of each word's meaning and intent, so it is mostly, though not exclusively, used in traditional Kirtans. In Kirtans, chanting is also called Bhakti or devotional yoga because it can help change one's focus from being mental to connecting with one's heart energy. All yoga is done for a reason, often to attune the physical body. In Kirtans chant verses are commonly repeated many times to deepen the energetic effects. It is seen that Kirtan chanting can shift those engaging in it to exalted energy states as the egoic and mental processes of the mind are minimalized. The receiver of this book had an incredible experience in it that converted her from hating it to loving it, and she now participates in it as frequently as she can.

In the United States, like much of the rest of your world, people have lots of opinions about prayer. Many commonly say God knows what is in my heart, that is what counts. That is what my receiver of this once thought too. Yes, God/Spirit/

Source does know what is in your heart, and it does count for something, but continue with me for more.

What is usually more important than God knowing your intent is that your body, as well as your heart, also know what your word choice energy is. Your body knows what you were feeling and where you were emotionally when you chose the words you chose. Even if you do not consciously know the energy of the words you express, your body knows it unconsciously and responds accordingly. We in the intangible realm cannot override your free will and so do not react to your thoughts alone. You must consciously ask us to intervene for you.

Consider the example of your curse words and who uses them. Just about everyone knows that cursing has a strong energetic effect. It can be positive in releasing a sudden pain or shock energy, for example. Cursing can also increase one's negativity and decrease one's energy when it is used frequently. Its negative effects are well known, that is why it is so widely criticized.

Also note that emotions are not feelings. Emotions are really your thoughts about your real feelings. So, the words you use are important because they are important to you. The English language has words that are used as both emotions and feelings such as happy and sad, making the important distinction between an emotion and a feeling difficult.

Distinguishing between emotions and real feelings is crucial. This is important individually, but it also reflects where your society is — what is important to you and your society.

Gathering with loved ones is a common experience for both unconscious and egotistical reasons. There is also power and unification within common goals in doing that.

Another physical example of where your world lacks understanding is its lack of interest in and understanding of the placebo effect. The power in it should be of great interest to healers, but it is not explored significantly in the Western medicine approach. There is more money to be made treating their illnesses and few people make healthy lifestyle choices. The placebo effect comes from an individual's expectations or belief that they will feel some effect. The fact is either positive or negative. Your fear of side effects may make you more likely to experience them even though you take the substance for positive reasons. The body knows where you are. That is part of why writers like Louise Hay have been able to write about different psychological effects on the body. Michael Lincoln's book *Messages from the Body* talks in depth about how lingering psychological effects affect the body many years later.

As is commonly shared, when two or more people gather, a unifying energy of a collective conscious "cloud" is created. A group's energy affects those in the group and others nearby. The collective energy affects those exposed to it.

Another example of that is called the 100th monkey syndrome. It is called that because it is based on the story on an island where a monkey was observed washing the food it was about to eat in a stream. Other monkeys observed that and discovered that washing the food items was indeed desirable. It was then observed that very soon after that monkeys on another island with no connection to the monkeys who started washing their food began to wash their food also. Before long, monkeys all over were washing their food.

If an individual, either through conscious growth or random accident, finds a solution to a concern and begins using it, others can consciously copy it. The real power is revealed though when others with no conscious contact with the original monkey, or individual, begin using the same tool or technique in a very short time without seeing it demonstrated physically. The unconscious energy transfer shows that there is an intangible effect that is very powerful. Research now shows that the energy transfer not only travels great distances (even unlimited is now believed), but that it does so at an infinite speed. It is commonly believed that light travels at the fastest possible physical speed. How intangible energies like thoughts travel instantaneously literally everywhere is not yet understood by your physical sciences.

Scientists know that things like light and radio waves weaken in proportion to the inverse square of the distance they travel. A star appears as a dim point of light in your night sky, but get too close to it and its brightness, its heat, will consume the physical you. It is no coincidence that if the Earth were a small percentage nearer or farther from your sun, life as you know it on the Earth would not exist. The key phrase is "as you know it."

Everything has a consciousness, there are conscious beings almost everywhere. Look to your science fiction writers and fantasy stories. Jim Henson's *Fraggle Rock*, officially for children, presented an important message for human society, namely that everyone is one with others. Your TV show *Star Trek*, and its sequels, include countless examples of someone's imagination, or imagineering as it has been called by Disney, coming about. The point here is that if you can imagine it, it can be done. Of course, it may take some time before it gets created physically. Your science and mathematics are catching up with people's imagination in terms of explaining how many phenomena occur. What is called a miracle is called that because how it happened is not yet understood, it is likely to be well understood eventually though.

Another example someone has written about is the transition from seeing something as a coincidence to later recognizing it as a synchronistic event connected with another event, to later seeing it as miraculous if you do not understand how it came about, but it happened at a fortunate time. Your imagination is limited by what you believe is possible. That is why your scientists struggle to understand things. In your earlier times people accomplished things not seen as possible in modern times simply because modern analytically focused scientists do not understand how different intuitive knowing is from mental knowing. Yoda in *Star Wars* illustrated that.

Those thriving in their heart connection and living as who they are often report that things happen that exceed their imagination, not just their expectations or hopes. The receiver of this has described such spectacular things happening several times recently. Yes, feeling connected with me and receiving this is an example of that for her.

You are truly an unlimited being, not physically constrained by your body. Have you heard of someone, typically a mother, doing something previously thought to be impossible to protect or save a loved one? You know that and other "miracles" happen.

Chapter 12

WHAT IS NEXT

Where you go with this is determined by you. From early in her life, my receiver wanted to connect with God as she heard others had done. She was told that anyone and everyone can connect and communicate with God/Spirit/Source. After her first vision where she felt called to prepare herself to serve others, she wanted to experience that again. Mostly, she has felt that she has yet to fulfill that calling even though she can tell you about many powerful experiences scattered throughout her life. Now, she can tell you about receiving this [*and preparing it for publication, and her life afterwards*].

I will share more information about my receiver in the hope that it will inspire you to a new awareness of hope and how much you are loved. Its inclusion in this book is your evidence that the receiver agrees to the disclosure of this information to help heal the world. With my approval, the receiver has changed some of the earlier sections to be more self-disclosing. The original message was intentionally vague with the expectation that the receiver could choose how much to self-disclose.

In the years after the receiver's first spiritual experience in which she felt she was told to prepare to be of service, she experienced many twists and turns, with many challenges in her life.

[At one point in my, Arica's, journey I was told that had the individual I was sharing my story with experienced any one of the major crises[11] I had experienced, they would have committed suicide. I have never seriously considered suicide although there was a time when I thought I was running out of options and considered that as a possible way out.

Arica acknowledges that during each of several crises the thought occurred to her that many people commit suicide in similar circumstances, but she always felt things would work out for her somehow. The one exception to that was the time that her brother was torturing her for being present in her family home where she had come to aid their dying mother. After their mother died, he began his torture by endangering her two dogs in a variety of ways. She told her brother that if he did not stop his actions and her dogs were harmed, she would kill him, then commit suicide since her life would be over once she killed him. His response was to intensify his actions. At that time, she knew that her two very loving dogs were what was keeping her alive

---

11 Commonly listed life stressors or causes of life trauma include: Death of a spouse or other loved one (including a pet), divorce, financial difficulties, loss of a job, marriage, having children, moving to a new area, rift with a close friend, and health issues. Arica has experienced all of these except death of a spouse.

during that extremely stressful period. She worried about what would happen to them if she was no longer around (and she would never harm them before harming herself). A friend reminded Arica that her brother's actions were illegal harassment. His actions ceased once she had a restraining order against him, so nothing more tragic occurred. Arica now recognizes that the miracle of her dogs not being killed, or even just injured, was through "divine intervention."]

After lots of other what she might call "semi-miraculous experiences," the receiver of this encountered A *Course in Miracles* (ACIM) book. She found that it did not speak to her in her expected language, so she stayed with her other resources.

[I had been in a metaphysics class years earlier and expected that God could and should communicate in modern language and would not need to use archaic Biblical-like language to appeal to Bible scholars or others with antiquated expectations of God. Now it seems strange that I rejected it only due to its language considering how drawn to learning more and connecting I have been. It may have been that I was not drawn to joining with others studying it. Lately, I have criticized others who stay with ACIM without at least examining its sequels. Also, I was surprised that my Life Physics metaphysics class teacher had not told us about it during his classes between 1976 and 1996. I expected he would know about it based on the wisdom and connection he demonstrated in many other ways and would then report about it to the class members. It was also surprising that none of the

students reported learning about it independently since we were
encouraged to also participate in traditional churches.]

Later, she [*Arica*] was introduced to *The Way of Mastery* book.
She saw it immediately as of value and appealing to her. For
reasons that she did not understand, she did not jump into it
beyond her introduction to it for several months. Then in a time
of openness and need, she went back to it and opened her heart
to it. She then read it almost nonstop over several days. More
recently, she has joined groups reading and studying the other
ACIM sequels I have dictated, *A Course of Love, Journey into the
Unknown,* and *Soul in the Driver's Seat: A Course in Miracles for
the New Age*. Next came her introduction to written messages
from others who have connected with me, and other divine
energies. Now, she has opened to me as she admired Rasha
doing with *Oneness* and *A Journey to Oneness,* and as others
have done with me.

My desire here is that you know that I and other divine
beings are ready to serve you anytime. All it takes is for you to
ask us to come in. Due to your free will, you must ask us to come
to you. Ask with the expectation that we can and will come to
you. Again, asking is crucial. We do not just read your mind or
otherwise violate your free will.

Additionally, as you [*Arica*] have been instructed [*by
Judy (Jude) Junghans*], who leads the book groups you have
appreciated so much lately, and which have helped to bring you
to where you are, it is wise to not ask for something specific but
say: "Legions of angels, masters, and friends, I request the most

benevolent outcome to this situation." Change "request" to "ask" and add their name if you are asking for another person.

Many have written about the ego in such negative ways that many believe their goal should be to kill it. Please let go of that concept. The ego is physically [*not eternally*] present in you for your benefit. Its purpose is to protect you. By alerting you to physical feelings it will protect your body, which you no doubt want, or should want. The difference is that in your world, the dangers are so well disguised and in different forms that they are rarely equivalent to danger coming in the form of a hungry predator ready to eat you or trying to protect its young from you. Instead, the energy of stress is often found in less tangible ways and then gets interpreted by the body as almost constant. Ongoing stress on the body overloads and damages it. The key is that the ego or mind is to serve you rather than control you.

That is why in non-medical language the heart is spoken of in reverence. When you let go of striving to control, as the ego and mind do, you open yourself to so much more, such as receiving communications from dimensions beyond your three-dimensional world. Intuitive knowledge will always uplift and encourage you, lifting you beyond survival and comfort into joy and peace. Happiness is your birthright, do not settle for less.

You have the expression "life is a journey, not a destination." That is very true. There is no end or destination. After all, you are immortal. Physical life is indeed a journey, but what does that mean? Is there no destination? In its widest context, it means that you are journeying to discovery of who/what you are and then living as who you are, an eternal individuated expression of

God/Spirit/Source. Since you are eternal, there is no endpoint, no destination to get to. It is most certainly not to a destination of heaven or hell.

Remember that there is no time perception in eternity; time exists just in the three-dimensional physical world. Yet, you hear some correctly say there is a soul's goal of growth. That means change. Change is constant even though things sometimes are happening at a slow pace, but other times they seem to be happening at a very rapid pace. Even in the eternal perspective, change is constantly occurring. Creation never ceases and so that is a constant change as souls are constantly growing in awareness.

Words trying to explain the intangible always fail. Have you tried to write or tell another about an incredible experience you have had? The common expression is "words fail me." That is because words do indeed fail you. They have their energetic value that cannot begin to capture the fullness of the energy in your experience.

Stopping here with the journey/destination discussion is not likely to be totally fulfilling; it probably does not satisfy all your concerns. What more is there? You probably imagine that surely something more could make it more understandable. There are video depictions such as *The Matrix* movie trying to portray life as though it is just a game controlled by some super controlling consciousness. In one sense God/Spirit/Source is a super consciousness, but that misses a big part of reality since you are a part of God.

It must be explained that you are as much a part of that super consciousness, and that it never tries to control you! In fact, it must wait for your clear invitation/request for it before it takes any action for you. That is why you must look within, find out what you are and be who you are — be all that you are. But what holds you back? Nothing other than yourself. Some of you have become more aware of how you hold yourself back. Limiting beliefs and self-talk using words such as "should," as in the expression "do not should on yourself," certainly refer to your limiting yourself. Another expression is that the real journey is from being mentally and emotionally centered to being heart centered — from head to heart is the longest, hardest journey.

Why does this matter? Simply because you are Love. Are you not expressing yourself as love, and feeling love coming to you? If you are not joyous, fulfilled, etcetera. in your life, what is the point? Being joyful, being love incarnate is the destination. And yes, you can get there and continue to grow in awareness. Perhaps, another analogy will help you understand this more clearly.

Goals change. For example, what brings joy to a child changes as the child grows. Consider a child that has one "goody" and is given another. The child realizes they now have more, or two, "goodies" depending on where they are in understanding numbers. Their joy is greater. As the child matures, what brings them joy changes.

Now consider more complex goals. Having used science and mathematics to reflect growth and understanding of increasingly complex issues, consider this: Is the sense of achievement significantly different than the child's when a scientist/mathematician realizes that they have achieved a significant goal? The physicist's ultimate goal might be to develop an equation that explains and unifies all the known forms of energy in nature [*electrical, magnetic, gravitational, nuclear, subnuclear, mass, thermal, chemical, etcetera, mechanical (motion), radiant electromagnetic, sound*]. What does that person get besides acknowledgement for that accomplishment from cohorts, friends, family, and perhaps awards and fame? Yes, the scientist/theorist has created something being sought by peers and may bring them great acclaim, but their inner satisfaction is not unlike the child's satisfaction unless their ego is out of proportion.

Remember Albert Einstein? Your technical world will acclaim anyone who surpasses what Einstein achieved. That person is likely to know that their achievement came about because they connected inwardly with some creativity or knowing deep within themselves and beyond their usual knowledge.

The same type of accomplishment can come from within you. And note that the level of fulfillment for you does not presume that you make a comparable earth shattering or changing leap of knowledge. Your response will be in proportion to where you are in your understanding.

You are where you are for reasons of your own choosing that you will eventually understand. A clue to where that will come from is in the wisdom of Albert Einstein. One of his well-known expressions is "the consciousness that created a problem cannot solve it." Less well known is that Einstein was quite spiritual and shared extensively with Ernest Homes, mentioned earlier as the founder of what has become known as the Centers for Spiritual Living (CSL).

The challenge of identifying what seems fulfilling and works globally is no small task. My receiver experienced this through the receiving of this book and now how her life will change as she gets it out publicly. The receiver left a successful career in the technical world about 1997. She has contributed to advanced research on the cause of climate change and other areas. She has made a number of what felt to her like major technical [*chemical instrumentation*] contributions to the world and made many personal changes during her life.

Imagine how frightened she is now bringing this out. She was initially fearful of self-disclosure, but as she felt my continued presence with her, she amended the text (with my guidance and approval). What you have here in this book, is her being much more vulnerable. For those who are close to me, they too are kind and loving. Remember the Bible quote included in Chapter 2, 1 John 4:6 – 7 shares that God is Love and that those who judge, and are hateful and persecute some, know not God for they do not live Love.

Many, however, believe that their version of belief in me is the truth and that it tells them that Arica is a devil to be exterminated, rather than her being Jesus' messenger; she cannot be exposing evil in the world for Jesus through this book. Some could choose to do her harm just for her daring to say I speak through her or that she speaks for me. Religious leaders have been known to kill their opponents in the past. Why do you think that that does not happen still, either by undercover official actions or by unauthorized zealots? Then there are those whose wealth and power in your world will be threatened by these words. How many can you identify from this book? Know assuredly that for everyone you can identify as being angered by this book's calling them out, Arica knows of them and more. Her just being a transwoman puts her in the most threatened minority in the United States. Here, she has cared enough for the Truth to get out that she is now publicly admitting that she is "one of those" since she knows that by making herself vulnerable, it increases her credibility (as well as risk). The probability is that the notoriety will help get word of this book and its truths out to more people.

You are not likely to be asked to take such life-altering steps. You can find happiness by ironically stepping out of your comfort zone. Would you love to hear me call out to you? To connect with you? Well, it is up to you. Just BE yourself. There is no doing to be done. The challenge is in your accepting that you are like me, Jesus, nothing less, nothing more. We are truly just comparable travelers on life's journey. The only difference between us is the experiences we have had in getting to where we are, not who or what we are. I will work with you to help you; you are like me and will help me best by helping yourself. There is no real difference between us.

Chapter 13

MORE ABOUT RELIGION AND ITS LEADERS

Receiver's note: Well, Jeshua, as this has progressed, I have had questions and even doubts about where this is going and if I was truly transcribing you, Jeshua, adequately. I feel like there is something coming here beyond what I could or would say or write by myself. I thank you Jesus/Jeshua, for giving me an opportunity to help change the world in a positive way. There has been so much negativity lately. I hope that what I contribute helps the world. Now, I yield back to you, Jeshua.

Rather than doubting yourself, how about letting in that I have been trying to reach you for some time. See that you are now more ready to let in my message than you think. I am closer than you can imagine and am just waiting for you to open your heart to me. I remind you to not think or believe that only certain people in days long gone communicated with

God/Spirit/Source. Some still teach that I can only be reached through them. Fortunately for you [*Arica*], your family's church taught you that you can connect and so you have sought connection throughout your life. You were launched on a quest for lifelong connection with God/Spirit/Source as many others have been.

The words here can lift and inspire you [*readers*] whether this is, as it is purported to be, from Jesus/Jeshua ben Joseph does not really matter. Look for the truth in this within your heart, your intuitive knowing, not in some so-called truth someone tells you to believe. Your heart, when you connect without confusion caused by egoic, or mental thinking never misleads you. Your heart is the best judge as to whether this message will serve you. You are my audience. It is for you.

You know that you deserve and have been wanting something more personal than a book claimed to be written almost two thousand years ago. You also know that what has been written is adulterated with things added in and other words of wisdom left out because what was written in them did not match with someone's goals for controlling others. Is God/Spirit/Source still alive and capable of communicating with humans? Of course! If not, God would not be God! God/Spirit/Source either exists or does not exist as those who have not experienced God claim. Even your wise scientists know there is a creative energy in the universe that is beyond human understanding. By letting this in, you are letting yourself find the answers to the questions you and many others have had for ages. Asking genuine questions is how you grow in understanding; questioning is not blasphemy as some would have you believe.

The information about what God/Spirit/Source is and how to connect has been greatly distorted over the centuries since my well-known life. First though is to acknowledge there is no written word directly from me, Jesus, also known as Jeshua from my lifetime. All written of me in your *Bible*'s *New Testament* was written long after I was gone and was each writer's recollection of their memories of me, or verbal stories they heard passed down by others about me after many years had passed. Then, of course, came the numerous edits, deletions, and additions as individuals either felt like some point or writer was too controversial and had to be removed or changed to suit their desires. Biases against certain ideas or perceptions were most certainly added.

Yes, there is controversy. Some, in seeking power, have tried to make it feel complicated and nearly impossible to connect with me, with God/Spirit/Source/Holy Ghost/Lord or whatever name(s) you choose to use. They convey that they are needed as an emissary or even that they directly represent me and what they say is gospel.

For example, early writings made no mention of LGBTQ+ people by that terminology or in any other words referring to such people; yet very strongly worded antithesis to love verses were added. A former Baptist minister and his father, a retired Baptist minister, studied the earliest writing that became a part of the *Bible* looking for where the admonitions against LGBTQ+ individuals originated. Their conclusion was published in a book[12] that essentially said that there was nothing to be found in the earlier writings that became the *Bible* that resembled in any way, or in any reasonable translation that could be interpreted as even a reference to gays or lesbians, much less criticism of them. Their interpretation was that the verses used to condemn gay and lesbians were added centuries later. They also identified a verse that referred to a beloved king and his queen who was probably a transgender woman.[13]

Why was hatred added to sacred scriptures? Note that in modern times many who do not accept themselves are often the most opposed to acceptance. It is called reaction formation by therapists.

Also reflecting prejudicial perspectives, the Jewish culture I was around did not accept women in leadership roles. Yet, Mary Magdalene was my best disciple. She understood everything I shared quickly. She was certainly not a prostitute as portrayed by many. The male disciples reluctantly accepted her tutorage and yet tried to compete with one another. It was not at all in accordance with the energy of love and acceptance I attempted to convey to them and others. It was a travesty of justice then and aspects of it continue now. My message has always been to love one another, to not judge one another, and to help one another. Now, it is being twisted into exactly the opposite of what I taught by some.

In contrast to what is being done by Christians, my so-called

---

12   *Hide or Seek: Re-Examining What the Bible Says About Homosexuality* by Jon Durre.

13   Arica has misplaced that verse's location, so it cannot added here.

followers of what I taught when I was physically on your planet, there is a wealth of wisdom in the so-called non-Christian new age movement groups and others. There, I can expect to find acceptance and followers of what I have taught. How about judging organizations and the values taught in them by the degree they help others, not how they help themselves and keep their members afraid to leave them? Hindus often chant "Hare Krishna" (Christna) which can be very loosely translated into calling in Christ consciousness. And no, Hindus do not worship multiple gods as is commonly portrayed; they acknowledge there are many (infinite) aspects of the one God that they then portray as a variety of individuals representing aspects of God.

Yes, there are indeed organizations trying to uplift people. Some make no claim to be Christian because being Christian has been made into a derogatory term. What is closer to being as I taught is being made into a so-called negative woke status.[14] Those studying my communications including *A Course in Miracles* and its sequels are far more Christ like than evangelicals, born-again Christians, Christian nationalists, and those with similar beliefs who label ACIM students, etcetera as non-Christian. Many religious leaders are more likely to call my modern followers devils or the devil's tools. This book is all

---

14   Woke status as defined and used here is caring about others. Those opposing a woke status seem to see it as a negative quality ironically about those caring for others mostly of different races or nationalities. That is not a true Christian value even though those opposing being woke claim to be protecting Christian values. Why do they fear and hate ones not like them so much? What are they afraid of? Have they forgotten the good Samaritan story?

too likely to be similarly labeled by similar belief groups. [*See Chapter 8 for more information on this topic.*] And do not forget the world has other peace-loving religions such as Hinduism and Buddhism.

Do I sound angry about what I say others who claim to represent me are doing in my name? My receiver of this knows that almost all who call themselves Christian, would reject her, and worse, because of her writing this, and other misconceptions they have. Instead of listening to those who come to model Love as she has, and to inspire acceptance and honor who we humans are, they are sometimes even denied the right to exist [*killed*]. She is right in having fears about what the reactions to this communication might be by some. This is intended to inspire hope that brings about positive changes, but as has been noted, those in power resist losing their power and have many devotees to help them for favors they might receive.

Turning away now from what is wrong, imagine with me a society where everyone is valued, no one is seen as being better than or beneath others. People talk about an ideal society or "utopia" to be called Zion as though it is unachievable. It is possible and not only that but will be achieved with surprisingly little effort. Once those so clinging to power can no longer fool others and are treated no differently than anyone else, true equality will reign. And yes, those who have had power and wealth are souls who deserve compassion. They can find proper roles in a true democratic society where there is equality for all. After all, what truly needs to change is for the United States to be a true democracy as envisioned in the founding of your country but sabotaged by those protecting their individual power. It has been said that the only hell is what is created within you. Heaven on Earth can and will be soon [or *eventually depending on when awakening consciousness occurs*].

It is not democratic when some place themselves far above others. A recent example is an individual demanding to be paid annually nearly what is being spent on aiding another country in its battle with an invading country. Would it be considered democratic and just for each to receive in accord with the value of their real contributions? Yes, it should, and admittedly to be fair, no one should be paid drastically more than any others. In fact, it might be reasonable for those who labor and abuse their bodies with hard, physically demanding, or dangerous work, or who perform tasks no one else wants to do, to receive high pay. If someone has the mental ability to direct things, is that arduous work for them? That is not to say that those who are creative and advancing the world should not be compensated appropriately.

In the United States, getting accused of being a communist is a nasty label. These days more toss around the term fascist, with some acting as though it is now desirable and needed, but others as its being despicable. Neither is anywhere near the type of country or organization that I am talking about here as ideal. Let me add that being called communist is technically inaccurate in that governments that have been called communist have never lived up to their promising equality implied in the true definition of communism; leaders have always set themselves up above others.

This is not intended to be a political manifesto, just a

questioning of whether there is any true equality or fairness in your system. This is intended to stimulate discussion about what equality means. Continuing in a controversial, thought-provoking vein, if wages cannot be equal for all, why not base them on degree of risk in doing the job, energy required to complete the job, or some other quantifiable criteria? Is that socialism? Is that so bad compared to your other options? It sounds fairer than capitalism as it is being defined and created by the ultra-wealthy these days, doesn't it? What makes some think fascism, contrary to the U.S. constitution, is okay?

Consider also how some of what is being done contrasts with what is being done in non-Christian philosophies such as Buddhism and Hinduism. There are many very spiritual beings in India, where Hinduism originated, as well as where the Dali Lama and his followers in exile from Tibet reside, for example.

The point here is to ask whether or not things being said and done in my name are really about bringing peace and happiness to the world. Are you prepared to contribute towards peace and happiness, not just for yourself, but for everyone and everything?

Chapter 14

CONCLUSION FOR THIS SHARING

Back to talking about Zion which is defined as being an idyllic community. That would be a community where there is justice, love, and support — true Christian values. Where is justice in a system where those stressed and troubled, or otherwise harmed in some way, cannot go to a therapist, counselor or other professional to get help (though currently what is available is not usually very effective and often requires many, many sessions for minimal progress). Providers may be doing their individual best, but their training has been influenced by less than altruistic interests.

Also consider that those with no resources to get professional help are often in desperation forced to self-medicate. They are then judged and often even sent to prison for trying to deal with their stress by using illegal drugs. They are told that they are bad/evil rather than seeing that they have been harmed and are unable to get support to help them out of the trauma they have experienced. Their trauma is added to as they are forced to cope with a world that judges them for trying to survive by self-medicating. Of course, there is no justice in that. The irony is that self-medicating is often as, or more, effective in dealing with trauma than professional therapy. Where is the help for lifelong issues that started in childhood when a child misinterpreted something that happened to them and forms what is called a limiting belief and low self-esteem? With the right approach, such as regression hypnotherapy, the experience can be seen for what it was, a misunderstanding of life and change accomplished quickly.

The point is that true help is not usually available to those who need it. All deserve true help; all are eternal souls and deserving of support. No one is ever cruel and deliberately hurtful unless they have been harmed to the point of their feeling justified in harming another and they see no other option. All souls are here to express love. Some get so harmed that their survival strategies then hurt others when they see no other way to cope with their trauma. People who hurt others, things or animals are themselves hurt and need loving care and support. How do they get it when the system does not even support the medical care some obviously need? Why is it that in the United States, one of the most developed countries, not everyone can get access to needed medical care, much less other types of assistance, to help them? Your system tends to judge people, not help them.

So where do you go if you agree with the thoughts and principles here? It has looked bleak, but it is about to change. Note again the vision my receiver reported having on November

7, 2016, about a healing period coming. The forces leading to control by powerful leaders will not continue much longer. When those in power lose control and others deceived into supporting those who had control and voted against their own best interest, wake up to how deceived and gullible they were, things can and will change quickly. Remember the 100th monkey syndrome. The pendulum swing back to reasonableness will be swift and decisive. The trend over your past 40+ years (90+ by some reckoning) towards the powerful gaining more power will be reversed far faster than many imagine.

Initially, there is some risk that change could come so fast and anger over what has been done lead to some revengeful actions. Revenge, of course, is not Christian. The powerful know of their risk and have managed to insulate themselves pretty effectively. Full restitution may initially seem harsh to those wanting to be fair-minded and balanced though.

Should the needs of the many be sacrificed for the few? This question was explored to a fair depth in your *Star Trek* TV programs and movies mentioned earlier. There the question was rigorously debated. That one does not harm another is a principle mentioned earlier. Is it truly harming another to be expected to give back some or even all of what they gained unfairly? The answer seems simpler when the question is reduced to are they going to give back what they got unfairly or is it harming them to have them undo the injustice that allowed them to gain so much?

I have no doubt that you can answer those questions fairly. Remember what is simple is not easy often. That is especially true when it is being approached mentally, not heart centered. The outcome will be worth the effort. The outcome will bring joy, happiness, and yes even prosperity beyond expectations to your world. And not just beyond your expectations, but beyond your imagination, way beyond it. Bringing you and the world joy, peace and happiness is God/Spirit/Source's intent. Remember God/Spirit/Source is God/Spirit/Source and so the goals will be achieved; Love will ultimately prevail. The only cost is your delayed joy if the timing is slowed. Ultimately, joy will reign.

Going back to the story about the type of governments needed, I acknowledge there has never been a major government or society in your modern world that lived up to the principle of true Christian values. Some nations have had powerful leaders but there has never been powerful countries that were truly peaceful in your modern era. All that were power focused were afraid to even try and see what would happen if there was no strong leader or central government. Those accepting the *Book of Mormon* know how far the American continent's residents got following my brief visit there after my crucifixion in Jerusalem. The 1,000-year *[meant to indicate an exceedingly long time, not a precise number of years]* time of peace and prosperity that followed my visit shows peace can be obtained quickly. Just because there is no example in your modern world, does not mean it cannot be done. The closest example of what you have any record of is in ancient times when there was a wise ruler, King Solomon. King Solomon guided things with wisdom, not a desire to control.

There is always the temptation for religious leaders to become corrupt. Look at what so-called Christian nationalists are trying to do these days in my name. There are no Christian values such as fairness and justice in them that could lead to a true democracy or peace. Remember God/Spirit/Source is creative enough to see solutions that do no harm to anyone or anything. With effort, humans led by their hearts can find those solutions. There should be no doubt!

Yes, humanity and even Americans can come together to create something beautiful. Your country was founded by people with a vision of an ideal government based on the flaws they saw in the countries they came from and knew of. They lacked some awareness of how they could be fairer and break away from the injustices they saw and had to compromise over, such as some of their peers holding slaves. But look at the beautiful start at something new your country had. Those injustices tolerated initially have gradually been eliminated, at least officially. Women can now vote and hold offices; slavery has been abolished. Many hearts remain closed and deceived at this time, however. With love, your country can be properly directed and restored to a symbol that gives not just hope but joy to everyone under it and it can again be a model for the world. All you must do is watch out for each other, take care of each other.

And yes, I am telling you being woke is a positive, not a weakness. Being woke should be caring about others. How can anyone think that is contrary to what I taught when I lived so many of your years ago. And if there are those who doubt this can be done, think of how quickly people promising change were able to take over your government and nearly succeeded in changing it into a cash machine for themselves. They were able to deceive millions who simply wanted to believe that change is possible. Unfortunately, those deceived got the opposite of what they and others wanted. Positive change can and will come about though. The only question is when it will come.

This is in many ways an indictment of religion in your world. Be willing to go back to looking within yourself as the *Bible* directs: that if you have questions, search and ask for answers and answers will be given to you. The shift I am advocating is to search within yourselves; do not expect a religious leader to be the one who gives you the best answers. Look within the Catholic Church, as an example. See that overall, Pope Francis of the Catholic Church is doing some good work even as others in it are doing all they can to stop his changes and bring the Catholic Church back to where it once was. In other words, some are trying to maintain their control even though they are not its highest authority. Restating for greatest clarity, the latest Pope has tried to foster greater love and acceptance, yet some do not follow him. They do all they can to subvert his changes.

Review question for Jeshua: There have been many topics covered here, many of which are quite controversial. It seems like others' recently channeled works are quite long. So, my question is, is this near to the end as I perceive it, or is it just starting?

You are correct in seeing that there is an endless number of topics this book could cover. You are also aware of your limits and what you can get out in a reasonable time. So, I will leave it to you to reorder them and see if these contain any glaring omissions that can be added without over tiring you or overly delaying it being shared. You have good judgment, and I will be with you as you proceed to the next stages for this.

Most of what has been discussed has been focused on the United States. There is also much strife in other parts of the world with active wars going on in Ukraine and the Middle East where there are accusations of war crimes against both sides. There is also strife in other parts of the world such as the Sudan leading to great pain even though those areas get less U.S. news coverage.

The principles I have given you here are valid everywhere, and like the 100th monkey syndrome, when you work out peace within yourselves and your home country, you will affect the entire world. Your individual efforts towards fostering loving one another and your planet will rapidly travel throughout your world bringing peace to all in your world and beyond. Again, you must only seek peace within yourself. That is all it takes to change your country and the world. It is no more difficult than that. You [Arica] found me, now experience my peace; others can and will do that too.

Is there anything else that I need to do now? Did I close here prematurely?

You have done well. Know that I will do as promised at the beginning and will give you the help you need to read your scribbling of my words down quickly and the help you need to move this forward. You have endeavored to be a great scribe for me, and I need sensitive, courageous, willing-to-listen scribes to move my messages forward to reach more people. That is why I am working so much with Richard Greathouse who is being assisted by Christina Strutt to bring forth ACIM sequels *Journey into the Unknown* and *Soul in the Driver's Seat — A Course in Miracles for the New Age.* [*They are currently only available online.*] Earlier ACIM sequels are: *A Course in Love (ACOL)* and *The Way of Mastery.*

Once you go through what we have created here, Rachel Jane and Datta Groover, Founders of The Awakened School where this book was received initially at a business writing retreat, will guide you well in determining how to proceed although they are not your only options. What else would you like to ask about?

Well, there is always my book I am nearly finished with now with just adding in quotations on even numbered pages as I felt guided to do. How will it be promoted and accepted? How does all this fit into my work and relationship with Steve?

Steve and you will be OK. He is in your life now for a reason, knowing subconsciously, at least, that this was coming. Review what I told you earlier about your other book.

What is the gift of this book? Why is this so much shorter than ACIM and its sequel books? Have I failed in receiving it?

This is not meant to be a book on spiritual or religious doctrine. It is a call to action, a call for change, so it needs to be short enough to appeal to more potential readers as it addresses current issues in your country and the world.

It is also to give hope to you and others for your future. Whether the future is scary or not is up to you. *[These last two short paragraphs have been added to the preface in the beginning of this book as well as being kept here at the end of it.]*

See for yourself if hearing my story gives you as much relief, hope, and joy as it gave me when I received it, and it continues to give me now as I transcribe and prepare it for publication. It explained to me more about how my life has progressed than is written here. It is a culmination of my lifetime searching. Now, I am no longer searching, never finding what I sought. I am a Finder having found what I sought.

It scares me to put out these controversial thoughts, but it gives me a personal peace now, finally feeling, and knowing that I am connected with Jesus/Jeshua and God/Spirit/Source, or whatever name used to describe it. Left out of the writing are the many thoughts and feelings I had in completing it.

The words here can lift and inspire you whether this is as it is claimed to be, from Jesus/Jeshua ben Joseph, does not really matter. Look for the truth in your Heart. That is what matters!

AFTERWORD

During the receipt of this work I, Arica Ellen King, experienced a variety of feelings. Some of them are referred to in the body of this work, in the "conversation" with Jesus. Since then, it feels appropriate to report what I have experienced following the initial creation of my handwritten record of what was given to me during the writing retreat. Transforming the handwritten record into an electronic document has continued to be magical though also more challenging and time consuming than I anticipated. I will describe the technical processes used first and then the experiences and feelings as they progressed.

But before describing the process used to convert what was written down during the writing retreat and then converted into an electronic document file, I want to summarize the sense I felt during and following the process. Receiving this felt more like the reunion of two long separated best friends after a long period of being apart. It was not at all like a boss or some authority coming to you to give you an assignment you must do. Rather, it was more like one of the friends had a task needing to be completed and the other feeling that wow, that is important and is desperately needed, how can I help you, what can I do? I want to be a part of that.

That reminds me of a dear friend I have. Our lives took us off in separate directions and we seldom connected after many years. When I told her I had become engaged, she just knew, that I was in for a busy time and suddenly found the time to be the best bride's maid/matron of honor a bride could ever hope to have. She just knew what I would need and jumped in to help make my wedding everything I could have hoped for, not just exceeding my expectations, but even my imagination for how great it could be. Before it I thought the wedding could be at any of several locations that were offered to me for it. It turned out to stretch the capacity of the large church where we received tremendous support. Since then, my and my friend's lives have been back to our normal limited sharing due to our ongoing responsibilities, but with my knowing our connection could not be closer. The only mystery is how we will support one another next. The difference I see with my connection with Jesus is that he is always available; physical limits do not apply to him. Now that I have opened my heart more, my busyness will not keep him away.

Now to the specifics of how this book came about. The time since the original writing was done has been like the original time of reception in some ways, but with some significant differences. The processes used and feelings accompanying them will be described as seems appropriate to me since some readers may wonder how this work was created. Since the original receipt of the book was completed before the end of the writing retreat, transcription of the handwritten book began at the retreat. The first approximately 4,000 words were entered into a WORD document there.

When I returned home, I immediately told Steve, my new

husband, of my experiences at the writing retreat. Expecting and fearing his reaction would be that my taking on this new project would interfere with work needed in our new business venture, I was surprised at how quickly he shifted into being very supportive. **Our**, (emphasis added deliberately and appropriately since both Steve and I worked on the draft together once I returned home from the writing retreat) has resulted in this book you have before you.

The next step was for me to read my difficult-to-read handwritten book to Steve and my computer operating in its dictate mode. Steve watched for errors in the computer's transcription of what I read. We stopped and corrected the transcript being created frequently (typically every paragraph) in our learning how to use the dictate mode of entering text into the computer. That was a first for both of us. It felt like Jesus was with me in the reading of what I had written as he had promised to be since I had been so afraid that I would not be able to read my hastily written manuscript since even my carefully written words are difficult to read for me and nearly impossible for others. My sense of Jesus being with me was palpable. There was only one word I could not decipher, and it was marked for later review. Subsequently, every time I begin to edit the draft, adding technical book documentation pages, or dividing it into chapters and naming them, it was obvious to me that Jesus was guiding me.

Following completion of my reading the complete book to Steve and my computer, my next step was to read the draft and make corrections the computer's edit function flagged as needing spelling corrections, punctuation, grammar correction or other *similar changes. In reviewing the computer's suggestions, its suggestions were usually not correct or calling for leaving out many adjectives I felt were more descriptive, not less specific as the computer labeled them, so very few of the many suggested changes were made. It was obvious that many of the suggestions were due to the computer's editing capability not being sophisticated and so were not desirable.*

My next step was to read the entire draft watching for what I recognized as errors of meaning during the hasty transcription and missed in the initial transcription and editing, but not flagged by the computer. I made very minor adjustments of wording for clarity in a few places that may have been from the difficulty of rushing my writing of the handwritten first draft. Great care was taken to not change any basic meanings or the initial intent. At that stage, the one word flagged earlier was still undecipherable even in looking at it and its context carefully. So, it was left flagged in the original handwritten manuscript and not added to what has become this book.

The following stage was having the computer read aloud the whole document to both Steve and me. I followed along with it looking at the handwritten draft. We both felt that the book's message was amazing and very much needed by the world. Our commitment to continue to work to get the book published grew tremendously as fears of some individuals reacting dangerously to this book and Steve and me were minimized. This work is just too important and valuable for us to not trust Jesus' promise to guide and protect us.

Excitement of working on such a big goal and anticipation

grew, yet Steve's and my fears about running out of our retirement resources were still present. Seeing that this can bring us all we need as people show their appreciation for our getting this message to them outgrew our fears. Even desires to travel can be met as we take on going on book tours, etcetera. I have avoided Law of Attraction, LOA, work, and related prosperity focused promotions even though they are quite common, and my monetary resources have been on a survival level, not at all a comfort level. In other words, I needed what the LOA works promise. Evidently, a feeling of lack and needing or wanting more is a big seller for many people promoting LOA programs. That is not consistent with my understanding of how the LOA should work, however, and it is not addressed directly in this work.

Receiving this book feels like something to share with the world and our wanting to get it out to serve the world is our motivation. Its possibly sustaining us after its draining our resources to get it out is a bonus for us, not the reason for doing it.

In the years leading up to this I have been participating in several book groups, reading either channeled works from Jesus, from ascended masters, or about them. Books about the Essenes and Jesus being an Essene have become important to me including those that show the value of past life recall hypnosis since I have done that myself and had clients do it spontaneously. Past life regressions have been of great value for both me and my clients even though I do not accept clients who seek that as their primary goal.

My regression hypnotherapy training has undoubtedly been a part of my preparation for receiving this book. Jude, who leads the book groups I participate in, other than the one I lead, has been yielding to me even more leadership roles of the book groups the past year, or more. Now, since my announcement of receiving this book, my role has increased. As others look to me more, I feel the expectations placed on me as well as Jesus being present guiding me. My sense of capability is expanding as I know and trust that Jesus and the Christ energy is with/in me.

A sense of fear that others will expect more from me and want me to do more has occurred, especially when I was participating in another program led by those who sponsored the writing retreat where I received this book. The joy returned as I saw more clearly that what was being promoted was being ourselves and being truer to our Soul purpose rather than making money. I can clearly say now, as earlier in my life, my joy comes through serving. That was the message in my first spiritual encounter about 56 years ago. I abhor the thought that I might be seen as doing this for monetary gain. So, that might be a message for me to be sure to look within myself deeper. Since I am asking myself that question, it could also show I have examined my motives.

Following the experience of fear that others will expect more of me and that I have nothing more to offer, I have had more insights. Rather than feeling I have nothing more to offer, I have come to see that this book came from "nothing" and yet, has so much to offer that I expect it to change our world. Realizing that for some time Jude, who leads the book groups I participate in, and others have turned to me frequently to explain how emotions are thoughts about feelings, not feelings themselves, has shown me there is more I may have to share. I see now what I know and can write about might grow into much more. After all, the channelers I have been reading from have not created the clarity on this topic that I have known of since my participation in Life Physics classes that ended almost 25 years ago after my participating in them for 20 years. Others do seem to appreciate my explanations about the great differences between emotions and feelings. If that and this book are "nothing," who am I to say there is anything more I can contribute to the world. I have spent my lifetime studying metaphysics after all.

At a diversity and inclusion group recently, I saw how much fear there was from others in the room. I was not able to stay silent at the end and told the group about my work to bring this book, Hope: Jesus Speaks to Modern America and the World, that I had received and believed I could get it out and available quickly. I anticipate that will be repeated as my courage to speak up grows. I cannot say what else I might do though. Since everything is taking longer than I hoped it would, timing for anything is very uncertain.

Getting back to the one word I could not decipher in my handwritten draft, I admit that I have not figured it out yet. Considering how the writing retreat was managed and my extremely poor handwriting, my having only one word indecipherable amazes me. The indecipherable word and its sentence seemed to me not crucial, so I have chosen to exclude it and the few other words that gave it its context. The change seems very minor at this time though the word remains marked where it was originally written so it and its intent may yet be restored.

I hope the care used in attempting to transcribe the hasty and poor penmanship written down to one uncertain word in *receiving this work is seen as the level of maintaining the integrity of reporting Jesus' message to me that has been attempted. The original writing was not done in a careful, slow methodical way with the expectation of this becoming a channeled exact replication. While exact duplication was impossible since my writing it was hurried without an expectation that it had to be taken exactly as the thought came to me, every effort was made to make it as exact as my writing permitted, however. Every instance suggesting a deviation from what was exactly as in the writing was considered very carefully while remembering the writing was detailed, but exactly what came to me was not possible with the circumstances at the writing retreat.*

My hope in your reading this is that it not only builds hope in you and inspires you to do more for yourself, our country and world, but in a more personal sense tells you that you are not unlike me. You can receive guidance from Jesus/God/Source/Spirit also. You too are a Christ, whether you know and express it or not. Everyone has intuitive knowing. Whether or not they know it consciously is the variable.

A key lesson I have learned is that seekers seek. It is when we discover that what we have been seeking has always been within us that we find true joy and connection. It has become a bit of a fanaticism of mine to emphasize that seekers are always seeking, never satisfied. Be a finder of what you want, not just a seeker of it. Self-labeling is important.

[Added after main text had been received.] I am ready to receive any more and act on your message now.

Yes, you understandably have fears of what haters might do to you and Steve. Know that I am with you and will protect you as needed. You will be doing so much for the world that is desperately needed. I love your stepping up to help me help the world.

MORE ABOUT THE TIMING OF THIS BOOK

This chapter was written by Arica regarding the timing of this book. being released. It was added following Arica's realizing that preparing the manuscript for publication had taken her so much time that getting this book out in September, as she once thought would be possible, or even October 2024 can not be done. Earlier sections discussed the potential timing of the coming great healing. Arica's hopes for getting this book out prior to the November 5, 2024, U.S. election in time influence its outcome could not be achieved. After realizing she could not get this book out in time to influence the election, Arica realized that could be a good thing and wrote the following.

Attempting to get this book published and available as soon as possible has proven to be more difficult than expected. I should not have been so naïve in my planning. I had already encountered numerous delays in getting my earlier book, How to Change: Finding and Moving into L.O.V.E. (Living One's Vital Essence), *finished and published by Balboa Division of Hay*

House Publishing. They are still waiting for me to send them the manuscript. I have had a contract with them for about three years and had thought I had finished the book other than adding the supportive quotations when I received this book. Selecting and positioning the quotations in the earlier book is taking far more time than I anticipated. What I am learning from this project will help me improve the earlier book before I finish it.

Now, facing the fact that this book will not be available before the November 5, 2024, U.S. election, much less being out in time to influence its outcome, it seems appropriate to add my updated perceptions regarding its publication timing and the timing of its message.

While receiving the book through Jesus, it was apparent he was resisting giving me specific timing and kept using the word "soon." It now appears obvious that Jesus knew that getting the book out in time to influence the election was impossible; it now seems it would also have been unwise. It was only my eagerness and hopes to affect the election outcome that led to my not realizing that it was my wish to try to change the election outcome, and not the intent of Jesus. After all, how likely is it that a book from an unknown like me could change the outcome of the election so fast? Oh yes, I am overlooking the power of God in writing that.

Realistically, I should have realized that it is obvious that there has been minimal healing of the hatred and divisiveness in the United States, or the election's outcome would not be in doubt, and yet its outcome is very much in doubt. I am not going to go back and modify what was written earlier about the timing of this and how the word "soon' is used. To do that would only delay this getting out even longer. I do add here that upon reflection it feels more likely that our country still has a great deal of healing to do. If this book came out earlier and influenced the election, the result would probably be pushing the hatred and divisiveness into hiding and would have further delayed healing our society. This way, the election will be a better measure of where we are, how much fear still controls us.

Healing anger, fear, etcetera throughout the world is not a minor task. People will have to see the Truth and have time to reflect on it for a while before many hearts change (Ignoring the 100th Monkey Syndrome). Heaven on Earth will come, just not in 2024 is my guess now.

What can be done to accelerate the end of fear and hatred in the United States and the world? It cannot and should not be attempted by trying to impose a different perspective on others. That is what this book attempts to remind us never works. Instead, consider that while some of us may disagree with how others see the world, those we disagree with are souls too. They too have what seems to them valid and even loving reasons to believe and do as they do. Ultimately, it is fear that holds us all back. Understanding and compassion are the only ways to help bring about positive change.

I am reminded of the time I was working towards my M.S. in Counseling. In my internship I was working with a family that included a 10th grade transgender student. The family was very supportive of their child and had attempted to legally obtain a name change for the child. The courts where we were at the time had refused to allow the name change even though the state laws had been complied with. The American Civil Rights

Union, ACLU, had taken the matter all the way up to where it was scheduled on the state's conservative supreme court's docket without success. There was fear that state supreme court would uphold the district court, and its ruling would then harm the rights of LGBT+ people statewide, not just in the conservative district involved. I was pressured to have my client family withdraw their suit to avoid risking LGBTQ+ people losing rights statewide. Having to continue living with and use her birth name that revealed her old gender would have devastated the young person.

So, what happened? I realized that the judge holding up the name change was really doing it because he thought he was protecting the young person. After all, protecting a child is a universal desire. The local judge was thinking like a typical parent, that he was protecting the child from misunderstanding parents. I wrote a letter to the judge explaining what I thought his motive was and letting him know that as the adolescent and her family's therapist, I could assure him that it was in the best interest of the child for him to sign the name change authorization. Without it, the risk of the young person committing suicide was very real. Literally the day the judge received my letter, he signed the name change authorization ending the name change legal battle and thus preserved the rights of others throughout the state by not having the case ruled on by the conservative state supreme court.

So, what am I calling for? Understand that all humans are souls who are doing what they believe is the right thing to do. Compassionately accept that and then assist them to see the different perspective they need to see things in a different light without any implication that they or their motives are wrong. But, how do we do that?

Remember the 100th monkey syndrome example. When people sense a new and better approach to something, they open to it. If it is forced on them, they resist it. That is only natural. The most effective way to help others is to love ourselves. As we learn to go deeper and deeper into loving ourselves, our energies reach out to everyone, uplifting them too.

I love sharing the example that for my book waiting to be published after this one, I chose to use the acronym L.O.V.E. for "Living One's Vital Essence" as part of the title for the book. In effect, the universe told me I could not use that acronym until I first loved myself more and then let love in from others. I was guilty of not doing either of those well earlier. I had thought that courageously accepting myself as a transgender woman was loving myself. It turns out that was only a small step in my loving myself and why I had come to life on Earth. Long after my realizing that, I was still living as though I had to go through life alone, never trusting that others would be there for me.

As you read earlier in this book, my other book is still to come out; I got married on March 16, 2024, part of why its publication was delayed. I believe that exemplifies how the universe works. I certainly beat the odds. Most of my friends have been single women and nearly all have given up on ever finding a partner. As a transgender woman, I had far lower odds of finding a partner. Who is still single? Not me, I have a wonderful husband who amazes me at how caring and supportive he is. Working with him to get this book out shows me how special he is. Remember what I and Jesus have said about him earlier in this book. As I learned to love myself more, love from him and others came to me (or I just started seeing what had always been there).

In the case of politics in the United States, understand that there is a great divide between the political parties. Assume though that everyone loves their country and wants to make it better. Do we see how to protect and strengthen the country differently? Absolutely. Now, the challenge is to recognize what it is that we all fear and to then open ourselves up to seeing that since we all care, we just need to seek the best way to improve things cooperatively. Can and must we unite? Yes, the world needs us to do that. Do you want to experience peace and joy, Heaven on Earth? My guess is your answer is absolutely yes!

A great way to get there is a tool I was just reminded of very synchronously (the story about coincidences, synchronicity, and miracles is for another time) is as follows.

As mentioned earlier, Steve and I are not sure how this book can or will support us, and not deplete our resources as it has been doing as we prepare to share it publicly. Reminding us of this, we just heard of a situation in which an individual we know was trapped in a seemingly unsolvable business problem with another individual who was seen as being rather obstinate. The feelings our friend expressed were curiosity as to how the seeming unsolvable problem could be resolved and wondering how it would come about. The expression used to describe the dilemma was "I wonder how this will be resolved; I am curious to see how it can be resolved." It was reported that soon after the curiosity thought developed, something very unlikely happened that resolved the dilemma. It ended a large debt without any payment being required.

The message to us and you, the reader of this is to be curious, expressing something equivalent to "I wonder how this will work out." For the healing of the fears causing the divisiveness and hatred in the world, our minds cannot comprehend how this can work out. We must wonder how it can work out for the world and humanity's sake. How this happens is certainly beyond our mental capability to create it. Otherwise, things would be getting better, not far worse as they have been. It is not, however, beyond the capability of God. The energy that travels at an infinite speed for infinite distances can create beyond what our conscious abilities understand. The energy and the outcome of its use defy mental or analytical understanding. It is activated when something as simple as wondering how this will work out and curiosity are expressed. Do you remember how curious many children are? Curiosity and wonder lead to solving problems intuitively using what some call "God energy."

When enough people wonder how to heal our society, a solution will be developed. Remember the 100th monkey syndrome. Have Hope, as this book is named and is intended to inspire. My life has certainly transformed. Yours and the world can also.

And in closing, especially since more Bible quotations were not included in this book, I suggest you rereading 1 Corinthians 13. It has many of the truths mentioned here in disguised/vague language. Someday I may write about it.

And now in closing I offer this ancient Hindu prayer titled in Sanskrit "Lokah Samastah Sukhino Bhavantu":

LOKAH SAMASTAH SUKHINO BHAVANTU

May all beings everywhere be happy and free, and may the thoughts, words, and actions of my (our) own life(s) contribute in some way to that happiness and to that freedom for all.

(English translation)

Appendix 1

ABOUT THE COMMUNITY OF CHRIST CHURCH THAT ARICA WAS RAISED IN

This section was given in the flow of the book but has been moved to here as an appendix since it does not seem to be essential for the understanding or completeness of the other portions. It seems intended to satisfy Arica's concerns about how the church her family brought her up in has been severely misunderstood and how that attitude might impact her.

And for your [*Arica's*] sense of clarity and peace in how others think of your background, I insert here that the *Book of Mormon* came out through one who was not a part of the church now known informally as Mormons and formally as The Church of Jesus Christ of Latter Day Saints. As you [*Arica*] know, and others should infer, you approach things quite differently than they do. The Mormon church began as a subgroup led by Brigham Young after Joseph Smith, Jr., the founder of the original church was killed by a mob. Brigham Young led the subgroup to Utah. That group became known as Mormons and changed the teachings of the original church by introducing such things as polygamy and belief in eternal marriages. The church you were a part of and led to your road trip is now called "The Community of Christ" and never had such controversial teachings. It is in fact, somewhat progressive, as I too could be labeled now. Your main take away from that church was that God and I are still alive and do communicate with people, unlike many who think my involvement with humanity ended with the *Bible New Testament* era. Your wanting to establish a connection was the purpose of that trip. Now, you feel and know that has been accomplished.

[Additional history of Arica's connection with the Community of Christ Church, previously known as the Reorganized Church of Jesus Christ of Latter Day Saints. Note that the Mormon church's name is similar except for the first word, "Reorganized." Despite the disappointing pilgrimage for Arica, she did go on to being ordained in the church. She notes that the church emphasis was on the Bible verses that say essentially "ask and it will be given" rather than having an authority telling members what to believe. Eventually, Arica found that her beliefs had grown sufficiently different from those of most of the church's members, so she left it rather than trying to change others. She went on to having a wide variety of experiences including exposure to many approaches to metaphysics or new age/new thought philosophy as well as almost all traditional and non-traditional therapeutic approaches seeking answers to life's questions.

Appendix 2

ABOUT RECENT U.S. POLITICAL DEVELOPMENTS

This Appendix has four short additions written by Arica Ellen King and approved by Jesus. in response to specific political developments within the U.S. as this book was being prepared for publication.

Part 1: About the Presidential Debate Between Biden and Trump

[This section was written on June 29, 2024, after the debate on June 27, 2024, between Joe Biden and Donald Trump.]

Notice how fearful, panicked actually, many are after the poor debate performance by Joseph Biden, Jr., and lack of challenge to the repeated lying by Donald Trump during the debate. There is obviously no trust that what is in the best interest of the country will prevail. There is only fear and that is a mind-based or egoic-based reaction. As I told you earlier, know that what is in the highest and best interests for the United States and the world will come about. Expecting to know why things work out as they do or how or when it will work is rarely productive. Trust that all will work out eventually.

Part 2: About the Attempted Assassination of Donald Trump

Some have suggested/requested that a response be added regarding the assassination attempt against Donald Trump. You are reminded that nothing has really changed. Initially there was some hope that Donald Trump would become more conciliatory, but you have now had enough time to see that nothing has really changed. It has gotten worse from some prospectives. He may get sympathy votes because of the violent act. He, as well as others, claims that I protected him so that he could go on to fulfill his destiny as President of the United States again. Neither I, nor God under any other name, stepped against human free will in that or any other incident regarding him. The collective consciousness of your country, perhaps being demonstrated more technically by the voters in the United States who reflect the collective consciousness, will determine how soon the growth in consciousness will be seen in your country and the world. The time of prolonged peace and joy will come only after the consciousness grows sufficiently. The measure of consciousness is not significantly altered by individual events. Violent acts, and other violent things, show very low consciousness.

Part 3: The Withdrawal of Biden as a Presidential Candidate and Kamala Harris Becoming the Democratic Party's Candidate

The withdrawal of your President from his campaign to win re-election has certainly stirred up excitement from non-Trump supporters. Rather than claiming that is a victory, I remind you that Love will ultimately prevail so as was reported earlier, nothing significant has changed. It is true, however, that in your timeframe, diminishing the divisiveness and other expressions of hatred can quiet the hostility. If it is done as politics and not with genuine Love, it can actually delay progress if those filled with hatred are simply forced to go into hiding. So, continue to support Love as I taught two millennia ago and continue to do so through those who let me into their lives. Remember, the best way to help is to continue your own growth while knowing that your growth will raise the collective consciousness, and all will be aided much like the 100th monkey syndrome helps all.

Part 4: The November 5, 2024, U.S. Election Outcome

Many in the U.S., and much of the world, is in shock over the outcome of the election of Donald Trump instead of Kamala Harris. They fear dark times are ahead.

Is there any good news? Of course there is. But first be reminded that what is in humanity's highest and best interest outcome is coming about. How that can be requires explanation. Know though that the outcome was not influenced by God, Jesus, or any other divine entity even though the most benevolent outcome is assured. It is always assured, only the timing is uncertain.

Go back to what was said earlier in this book about a great healing period beginning. For healing to occur the issues must be accepted and understood. The November 5th election revealed that there are many voters of the U.S. who have great fear and even anger and hatred over what has been happening in our government. Of course, not all voters who voted a certain way did so for the same reasons. Some may have voted simply because they believe a change is needed, not because they are hateful towards anyone individually or any group.

The Democratic party leaders managed to prevent Marianne Williamson and others from challenging Joe Biden in a Democratic primary in 2024 and then quickly substituted Kamala Harris once Biden withdrew from running for the presidency again. There are other ways in which Democrats can be seen as less corrupt than the Republican party, but still corrupt. Some of those voting for Trump may have just voted for change that the Democrats had not brought in to benefit them. While few believe Trump will really bring in changes to benefit lower income people, voting for promised though probably false hope is more likely than voting with no hope. Humans are not dumb.

Given the divisive nature of much of the preelection rhetoric however, one can assume that many people are resentful of minorities, immigrants, and other groups of people. Now, it seems likely those attitudes are not going to be pushed into hiding. Rather, they may be expressed more freely. In their being expressed more openly, it will be easier to identify how to heal the underlying fear and anger. So that may help usher in the coming healing period.

Remember what happened January 6, 2021, at the U.S. capital. The violence that led to deaths there was threatened to be unleashed further if the election was "stolen" from Donald Trump. He certainly cannot claim it was stolen from him since has been acknowledged as winning it, and there appears to be no uprising likely in contesting his election. So, the election of Donald Trump may have eliminated the possibility of something as drastic as another civil war within the U.S. Not having a civil war or other violence seems likely to contribute to opportunities for healing.

So, nothing significant has happened to hamper healing. What continues to be needed is for each of us to see and acknowledge that we are Love, not its opposite fear. As we continue to grow in being Love, the collective consciousness will grow, and the healing will occur. Yes, it appears that the period of Heaven on Earth did not start in 2024, but that does not mean that it will not be soon. As more and more people learn the truths shared in this book and live them, peace will result. The energy will spread quickly as each person grows.

STATUS OF OTHER WRITINGS BY ARICA ELLEN KING

How to Change: Finding and Moving into L.O.V.E. (Living One's Vital Essence)

As could be expected from its title, it is about how to make deep, lasting changes in one's life. Childhood experiences almost always lead to the formation of limiting beliefs and a shadow side. Traditional therapies are so ineffective in changing them that many people believe they cannot be changed. Arica has learned how to change limiting beliefs quickly and shares how to do so as she teaches and models how to change and find happiness in life regardless of one's circumstances.

How to Change has not been published prior to the publication of this book. When she channeled this book, Arica was ready to do final edits and selection and positioning of supportive quotations on even-numbered pages of the main body of the book when she channeled this book and chose to work on it as her higher priority. It is expected to be published by the Balboa Division of Hay House Publishing within a few months of this book's release.

A Soul's Journey

A Soul's journey is listed here because Jesus mentioned it in this book implying to Arica that she should consider it more deeply. Jesus mentioning it may have been because the concept came through a rare moment of creativity at a time when Arica did not often express creativity. *A Soul's Journey* currently exists in a rough concept or outline stage only, with Arica having no current plans for how to develop the concept. It lacks many chapters even in outline form. Only a few chapters have even a rough start and Arica has no current plans for even how to continue the concept. The mention of the book and other clues suggest it may be developed eventually, when she feels more ready to do so.

Awakening Awareness: Who Am I and Who Are You

Awakening Awareness is a memoir or combination autobiography and self-help book. It has not been published nor has that been seriously anticipated. After writing it, Arica saw it as more for her than for other readers. It was written before Arica's introduction to Heart-Centered Hypnotherapy training. So much has changed for Arica since then that it requires major revisions or made into Part 1 of Arica's early history and a second volume possibly to be titled something like Awakening *Awareness: Who Am I and Who Are You*

Volume 2: Going Deeper being written. The effort to redo it will be made only if a demand for it develops from readers of *Hope* and *How to Change* wanting to know more about Arica's history and how she has become who she is.

Finding a Spiritual Connection for Those Who Do Not See Evidence of a Spiritual/Non-tangible Dimension

This started many years ago as a booklet when Arica was still working with many others in technical fields. Publication was never pursued.

Possible Future Writings by Arica

Since receipt of *Hope*, Arica is hesitant to suggest what might be next from her other than her finishing *How to Change: Finding and Moving into L.O.V.E. (Living One's Vital Essence)* as quickly as possible as directed by Jesus. Do know that Arica feels like she grows most when she is serving and so is likely to always be found pursuing whatever appears to be the most helpful for others. Arica Ellen means "Loving Light" so be on the lookout for a bright light wherever she is — and within you and others.

It does feel like there might be a call for Arica to elaborate on some of the topics barely touched on in this book. Examples Arica is beginning to recognize include as next topics include: thoughts and emotions vs feelings, gratitude, free will, Law of Attraction (LOA), and forgiveness. Of course, there are many topics only mentioned or not even unaddressed in this book that may become priorities.

The listing here is not intended to be seen as to be expected soon or even ever. It is only to say that there may be more to come, and Arica does not consciously know what is next after this book and *How to Change*.

ABOUT THE RECEIVER: REVEREND ARICA ELLEN KING

Arica Ellen King has been a lifelong student of metaphysics and self-development. As a young adult at her first church retreat, Arica had a life transforming experience. Arica was told by Spirit that she should prepare herself to serve. She went on to being ordained in the somewhat traditional Christian church now known as The Community of Christ. It emphasized searching for answers within oneself and not from authoritative leaders. Finding her beliefs and interpretations becoming increasingly different from most others in the church, she left it after a few years. After her departure from the church, her connections led her to focus initially more on psychological issues including teaching parenting classes as she pursued a technical career in which left-brain analytical thinking dominated. Moments of insight emerged during her technical career that led to accomplishments resulting in Arica's being listed in Who's Who in America and numerous other technical achievements not identified in this book. All of them were under her former name. She eventually connected with a "Life Physics" metaphysics teacher with whom she studied for about 20 years.

Leaving the technical world in her fifties, Arica moved into personal coaching and teaching relationship and self-awareness classes. That led to her going back for a Masters in Science in Counselling Psychology, then Heart-Centered regression hypnotherapy training at the Wellness Institute near Seattle, Washington. While personal coaching began opening Arica, what started at the Wellness Institute led to a period of deep personal growth resulting in her ultimately shifting all her Myers-Brigg personality profile scales. Arica became noted for her modeling that change is possible. While her gender change following her becoming a personal coach is recognizable and leads to her being seen as a model for change, it was the personality profile changes that really showed Arica that change is possible. Her gender change was simply gaining the courage to begin living as who she is.

Affiliating with churches and a wholistically focused non-profit organization following her counseling training to further her social connections, Arica refined her workshop and speaking skills. One minister at a well-known large church took to greeting her as "Oh Great Presenter" after her popular presentations to the women's group at that church. Since this book was received by her, she has sharpened her skills through working with the Toastmasters organization and The Awakened School's speaker training.

Arica's relevant formal credentials and training include M.S. Counseling Psychology, (Advanced) Clinical Hypnotherapist, Higher Alignment Personal Coach/Relationship Class Facilitator, Reiki Master (Lighterian and Usui Reiki), Crisis/Rape Counselor, Stress Elimination Technique (SET) practitioner. Arica also received training in: Radical Forgiveness, PSYCH-K, NLP, EFT,

EMDR, Voice Dialog, LGBTQ+ (especially transgender identity) issues, metaphysics minister, and Life Physics student for 20 years.

Prior to moving into the therapy world, Arica was a chemical instrumentation developer where she revolutionized several industries and became listed in Who's Who in America (under her old name) following her receiving M.S. degree in chemistry, physics, and science education (All but Dissertation [ABD] for a Ph.D. in chemistry). While those times she was mostly in an analytical/mental mode, those achievements came from what she now recognizes as her mostly unconscious intuitive connections.

Recent achievements include Arica becoming a popular speaker (having once been an extreme introvert and still considers her speaking skills as "improvable," publishing numerous articles in various newsletters, etcetera. The previous section has information about other publications Arica may yet complete.

Arica's focus recently was on building self-esteem and true healing by empowering inner strengths and wisdom by eliminating emotional blocks, self-limiting beliefs, and unconscious patterns of behavior using non-traditional tools which yield rapid results.

A major milestone for Arica was achieved just before the publication of this book and Arica's upcoming How to Change. *In Arica's writing the book using the acronym L.O.V.E., the Universe "required" her to go deeper in both self-love and accepting love. Love totally unexpectedly came into her life and she became engaged and then married as the quotations for that book were being worked on. Other incredible events continued before this book's manuscript was finished.*

See AwakeningSoulsLOVE.com or AricaEllenKing.com

ACKNOWLEDGEMENTS

Arica wants to thank Claire Sanders for her incredible work assisting her in preparing this book for publication. This book and working with Arica presented unusual challenges and Claire met all of them admirably. Claire's recommendations that I add more self-disclosure and other clarifying information makes this book feel more complete and adds to its message for me. I will certainly give Claire an opportunity to join me for any future projects I have.

Arica also wants to thank Mark Thomas whose creativity and expertise in designing the cover and interior formating/layout for this book were challenged by my strong preferences. He was very patient in explaining his recommendations and dealing with my numerous revisions.. This book is much better because of his work and assistance including his recommending Claire Sanders for the text review/editing.

.

God is everywhere,
everyone,
everything and
everlasting.
There is only God.

Made in the USA
Columbia, SC
15 March 2025

55184547R00080